Educating Christians

Educating Christians

The Intersection of Meaning, Learning, and Vocation

Jack L. Seymour
Margaret Ann Crain
Joseph V. Crockett

Abingdon Press
Nashville

EDUCATING CHRISTIANS:
THE INTERSECTION OF MEANING,
LEARNING, AND VOCATION

Copyright © 1993 by Abingdon Press

93 94 95 96 97 98 99 00 01 02   —   10 9 8 7 6 5 4 3 2 1

This book is printed on acid-free, recycled paper.

Library of Congress Cataloging-in-Publication Data

Seymour, Jack L. (Jack Lee), 1948–
    Educating Christians: the intersection of meaning, learning, and vocation/Jack L. Seymour, Margaret Ann Crain, Joseph V. Crockett.
        p. cm.
    Includes bibliographical references and index.
    ISBN 0-687-09627-8 (cloth: alk. paper)
        1. Christian education. 2. Meaning (Psychology) I. Crain, Margaret Ann. II. Crockett, Joseph V. III. Title.
    BV1471.2.S44   1993
    268—dc20   93-18583

Scripture quotations are from the New Revised Standard Version Bible, Copyright 1989 by the Division of Christian Education of the National Council of the Churches of Christ in the U.S.A. Used by permission.

MANUFACTURED IN THE UNITED STATES OF AMERICA

To loved ones,
who are gift, grace, and joy

CONTENTS

ACKNOWLEDGMENTS

Each of us has mentors and friends who have influenced us in Christian education. Together, we thank those who have read and commented on drafts of this manuscript: Cecile Adams, Sue Detterman, Charles Foster, Robert O'Gorman, LeeAnn Sinclair, and Meredith Underwood. They helped us clarify our meanings. We also thank our editor, Jill Reddig, and her colleagues at Abingdon Press for their insight, understanding, and encouragement.

Jack acknowledges his indebtedness to three friends: Charles Foster and Robert O'Gorman, with whom he worked for eight years, and Linda Vogel, his colleague at Garrett-Evangelical Theological Seminary. They provide support and stimulating conversation, exploring issues of the nature of the church, public life, and the praxis of education. He thanks Garrett-Evangelical for providing a grant which helped to support his participation in the research for this book. He also thanks colleagues in the Religious Education Association who are exploring how people work together across their differences, on fundamental issues of life and justice.

Margaret Ann began in religious education through United Methodist certification studies in Christian education and continued in a doctoral program at Vanderbilt University, where she explored questions of community and learning. The congregations of the Community and Missouri United Methodist churches in Columbia, Missouri, and her colleagues in ministry have provided rich experiences of people struggling together for meaning.

9

Joseph's first mentors in the professional field of religious education were Ethel Johnson, Grant Shockley, Charles Foster, and Robert Browning. They empowered Joseph to probe his own experience and education within the African American church. Colleagues at Colgate Rochester Divinity School, such as Walter E. Fluker and Don Matthews, are conversation partners who empower his work and call him to claim his vocation.

INTRODUCTION

On the occasion of his retirement, United Methodist Bishop Edsel Ammons, interviewed about the declining membership of mainline churches, said:

> Our focus needs to be on those crushing issues of life and death beyond the church, rather than on ourselves. . . . The greatest threat is not our loss of constituency (though lamentable) but our failure of focus and our investment in a discipleship without discipline, substance, or reach.[1]

The engagement of those crushing issues and our discipleship are tasks for the church's education. Religious education begins with the basic human need to make meaning. The church and its education fail when they do not take into account people's life experiences and their search for faithfulness.

Research for this book began as we listened to people who spoke about those crushing issues. They asked: How do I respond to crisis (death, illness, divorce, loneliness, oppression)? Can I hold my life together? How do we, together, seek meaning and purpose in a world that seems to be disintegrating? How do we contribute to a future of justice and community?

People are caught in the powerful experiences of dying and birth, conflict and community, brokenness and nurturing, pain and hope. Personal lives are disrupted. Life is chaotic. The whole world is chaotic. Even with the reduction of the nuclear arms race, fear and suspicion abound. The gap between the rich and the poor widens. Life itself seems tenuous as air and water are jeopardized.

Even education is chaotic. School leaders are forlorn about the direction they are to take. Many people lack hope, and society appears unable to address pluralism constructively. In some inner cities, as many as 60 percent of children drop out of school. Church education too is chaotic. Programs decline. Mainline Christianity seems increasingly privatized, not speaking to life issues. Old answers and traditional expectations are insufficient.

Individuals and cultures are searching for meanings that offer hope and inspire solutions. Their search is theological, asking questions about the nature of the future, of community, of being human, of salvation, and of God. These questions are ignored only at great risk to the future. People are empowered to live, to reach out to others, to build structures for community, and to find means to sustain and nourish others only by confronting those crushing issues of identity and vocation.

Religion is central to this public discourse about meaning, vision, and hope. Religions respond to the mystery, pain, and joy experienced in life by directing people to nourishing wells of meaning. Communities of faith teach their traditions and engage in critical theological and ethical reflection about purposes and actions; they are religious educators.

Religious education is thus grounded in life experience. People seek to interpret their lives in relation to God. At times, however, the church abdicates this search for meaning by communicating that it is a place for saints with no problems, instead of a place to heal and challenge those who are hurting and broken.

At other times, the church reaches deep into its reservoir to offer hope and community. And while these experiences of challenge and hope have too often been fleeting, the authors of this book have found them powerful. Glimpsing possibilities for meaning has called us to search for a religious education that engages life experience with the tradition, and with the passion of God's will for wholeness and justice.

Listening to One Another's Voices

While all three of us have worked in the church and taught religious education, we come to this study informed by three different perspectives: Jack is ordained and teaches religious education in a theological seminary; Margaret Ann is a diaconal minister of education, serving a local congregation; and Joseph is an ordained theological educator who also has worked on a denominational staff. Our ethnicity, our church experience, our gender, our professional life—all have contributed to the way we understand the struggle for meaning and the role of religious education in ministry.

In 1982, Jack co-edited, with Donald Miller, *Contemporary Approaches to Christian Education,* which provided a map for the field. Instruction, faith community, development, liberation, and interpretation were the metaphors discovered. The study raised questions about the commitment of Christian education to tradition, life experience, personal meaning-making, and social change. Later, with Charles Foster and Robert O'Gorman, Jack wrote *The Church in the Education of the Public,* challenging the increasing withdrawal of church education from public life to issues of institutional maintenance and survival.[2]

Both these books, along with experiences in serving a congregation, working on a project with churches in transitional neighborhoods, and contributing to curriculum for peacemaking, have led Jack to explore how Christian education links public life with faith. He comes to this book with a conviction that education engages people in theological and ethical reflection as they seek to understand God's call in their lives.

Margaret Ann came into Christian education as a second career, having taught communication skills to college students. When her father's death raised questions about the meaning of life that she could not answer, she experienced the failure of church education to meet people's needs. Later she worked as an administrator of those programs, tinkering with schedules, publicity, and topics, and found that they still failed to meet people's needs. She suspects that people are staying away from church school because it is irrelevant to their lives. Sensitive issues are often excluded from conversation, and pain is avoided. Her suspicions took focus one summer as she read Parker Palmer's *To Know As We Are Known* and found there a way to begin to express her deeply held but unarticulated understanding of teaching as space for living life's questions.[3]

Later, in a doctoral program, she tested that thesis. Yvonna Lincoln introduced her to the discipline of naturalistic inquiry.[4] That discipline, with its presumption that voices need to be heard and honored, felt so right. Using naturalistic ethnography for her dissertation research taught Margaret Ann that this way of being in the congregation (listening to stories and standing alongside those who are remaking meaning) is her way of ministry.

Joseph began to be conscious of the power of education in the early 1960s when his family moved to Shaker Heights, Ohio. At that time, the United States was experiencing significant racial tension. His was one of a few African American families to integrate their neighborhood. Even the supply of the latest educational resources could not cover the lack of attention to his people. His history textbooks contained only one picture of African Americans, and that was of men in overalls and women in smocks, picking cotton. Joseph's family had integrated the neighborhood, but their history was not honored. When his experience was made invisible, his history was marginalized. He was oppressed.

Coming from a long line of preachers, Joseph entered the church. He sought to preach, edit curriculum, and work as a denominational educator in ways that made people's experiences and voices visible. In the 1980s, he began a research project on education in African American churches. That study, *Teaching Scripture from an African-American Perspective,* showed that both faith and culture are engaged through the biblical witness.[5] Teaching scripture in the African American church means to "cry aloud," to give voice to one's historical and cultural experience. Giving voice to experience, listening to the words of the ancestors, and living a language we feel, think, and act upon is now central to his teaching of seminary students.

Writing this book has been difficult but satisfying for us. We have struggled to embody our convictions, even when we did not yet have names for them. We have worked to create a just and hospitable space for one another, communicating across gender and racial differences. We have sought to practice the presence of God. We have learned from one another, arguing, clarifying, and affirming. It was never easy. But the product of living those convictions is different from, and greater than, any one of us could have accomplished alone. Our experience in writing affirms our convictions about the mutuality of education.

Reading the Book

Texts on education focus on the content and practices of teaching. In this book, the theory and practice of

teaching are grounded in the ways people learn to
negotiate the terrains of their lives. Those of us concerned
about educating Christians enter a mutual and open
search for meaning. Together, we encounter new
experiences, respond to one another, address significant
life changes, and are called to new life by God's grace. We
ask *why* and seek to discern how to live. We learn in the
midst of the experiences of our lives. The education of
Christians is an intentional activity, in an open and safe
space, where profound issues of living are addressed.

This book begins by exploring meaning (chapters 1 and
2). We listen to people as they describe how meanings
shape their identities and vocations. Meaning is fundamentally a gift of God's grace (chapter 3).[6] Teaching and
learning must be grounded in the way each of us makes
meaning in relation to the Holy One.

The three middle chapters describe processes and
settings that empower people to learn. In chapter 4, we
examine the learning process. Then we explore how
religious learning takes place within the church (chapter
5) and in the world (chapter 6). Chapter 6 defines
education as an intentional effort to provide settings and
processes within which people can interpret life experience in relation to others, the faith traditions, and God.

The final three chapters move to the processes of
education. Chapter 7 describes teaching. Chapter 8
explores how religious-education leaders shape settings
for learning and teaching, and make decisions about
ministry. The Postlude then returns to the issues with
which this introduction began: How do we live meaningfully and faithfully in this world? Christian religious
educators have much to contribute in answering that
question.

Throughout the book you will meet people who are
trying to be faithful to God. You will also encounter

congregations and ministries that seek to incarnate God's presence and provide vision for our living and serving. We thank those who have invited us into their lives.

We invite you to explore your own experiences in light of their stories. To aid in that process, reflective activities are placed throughout the book. Each time you encounter an activity, take a moment to sit back and reflect. Explore your ideas and experiences in relation to the passions and convictions we have expressed. We invite you to journey into the ministry of meanings, toward religious identity and vocation.

If you are a pastor, we hope you will assume your role as educator in the midst of people searching for meaning. If you are a Christian educator, we hope you will find words to express the convictions the practice of Christian education has taught you. If you are a student, we hope you will enter Christian education honoring those alongside you who also seek to know God, to embody their vocations, and to share in the search for meaning.

Bringing deeply held and known-but-not-yet-articulated ideas to birth is painful. Sallie McFague's conviction that "no single voice or species is the only one that deserves to be heard" has guided us.[7] Our three separate voices have not easily become one, but we have tried to honor one another's points of view. We hope your voice will speak in the midst of the people as you hear their voices. We welcome you to the search for wholeness and justice.

PART ONE

MEANING AND FAITH

CHAPTER ONE

TEMPLES OF MEANING

The Search for Identity and Vocation

In 1971, a few weeks after entering the army, Travis declared that he was a conscientious objector. That action initiated an intensive effort to make sense of his life and values. The year before, Travis had spent a year in seminary where his value conflicts were highlighted. But at seminary the views of his mentor, a theologically liberal professor, radically conflicted with those of the Fellowship of Christian Athletes, whose support had led Travis to seminary. The conflict in perspective proved too much, and he left.

"I was bummed out," he said. "I realized I was in seminary for the wrong reason—to escape a military obligation—so I reported to the army." Travis described the declaration of being a conscientious objector:

> While I took some army R.O.T.C. in college, it had just seemed like a diversion, a nuisance. Yet, a couple of years later, when I reported to Ft. Benning, Georgia, I knew I wanted to make the best of it, do a good job. I guess I had the image of myself saying, "Follow me, men." However, after about three weeks of infantry training where we called in locations for bombings, I told my commanding officer, from that point on, I considered myself a conscientious objector. I respectfully declined to fulfill any

leadership position or carry a weapon. It just was not
consistent with everything I believed was right. Part of the
application for C.O. status was submitting a statement. It
brought into focus a lot of things. Once I made that
statement of faith, I felt I could never change it. It's no
good if you're not consistent.[1]

Those months writing his conscientious objector justification for the army were powerful for him. He faced a
crisis of meaning and experienced himself as a meaning-
maker. "They were asking me to be something I didn't
want to be and didn't feel like I had the capacity to be." He
learned much about his values.

Several years later, Travis faced another turning point
in his self-understanding as he separated from a mentor:
"When I first worked for Max, everything he said, I said,
'that's right.' I'd catch myself saying things that I had
heard Max say, and I realized that they weren't my ideas,
they were his, and I needed to start taking responsibility
for my own ideas."

Shortly thereafter Max died, and within a couple of
months Travis' father also died. Their deaths were a crisis
of meaning. Responding to the loss, Travis solidified his
own values and claimed some they had modeled: "I reflect
back on some things those men stood for and I want to
stand for too. Men with great commitment to wives,
families, hard work, honesty, who treated people well.
Hang onto your roots and the things that brought you
where you are today and hold onto 'em real tight."

Travis faced several crises: declaring himself a C.O.,
separating from mentors, and dealing with death. In the
process, he discovered and affirmed personal meanings.
He reclaimed his "roots." By seeking to make sense of life
and to discover meaning, he dealt with issues all humans
must encounter: identity and vocation.

Living in Meaning

Travis' story parallels the experience of many of us. The details are, of course, different, but as we live, we struggle continually to discover meaning in the midst of disparate events. We find those meanings as we tell others stories of our lives and express the beliefs on which we stand. Some experiences draw us deeply into what is called theology—that is, basic questions about the nature of the world, of God, of relationships, of the presence of evil, and of our life commitments. To be human is to dwell in, and live out of, meaning.

Metaphorically, we dwell in personal "temples of meaning." Our temples are vital to our existence. They provide support and protection. They are always under construction or reconstruction. External walls need to be shored up or enlarged, or furnishings rearranged. Sometimes our temple has soaring ceilings and stained-glass windows, representing grand narratives which provide meaning. Sometimes our temple grows dark; the windows are narrow and the floors become shaky.

The temple metaphor is illustrated in the words of a priest describing a Buddhist temple: "In every design you see—no matter how simple, how elegant—some tiny detail is left unfinished. This reminds us that human life is never completed. The workman can always come back and find more work. Your life, too . . . will never be completed."[2]

We dwell in, and live out of, these unfinished temples of meaning. They provide the perspectives through which we filter experiences and make meaning.

Meaning Arises from Encounter with Life

The stuff of which humans make meaning is experience, life. Educator Jack Mezirow asserts, "Our need to

understand our experiences is perhaps our most distinc-
tively human attribute. We have to understand them in
order to know how to act effectively."[3] As Travis declared
himself a C.O., he sorted and interpreted the myriad
experiences in his life to derive meanings, which, in turn,
guided his actions.

Meaning must often be remade. We are particularly
challenged when death—the death of a person, of a
relationship, of career expectations, or of dreams—shakes
up our taken-for-granted worlds. Robert Coles relates the
story of a young boy from the Appalachian hills at the
scene of a mine cave-in which had killed twenty miners,
one of whom was his father.

The boy asks, "Why does He [God] sit back and let that
happen—and those operators and owners, they won't
even apologize, and God must know they won't?"[4] This
question, flung in the face of evil and injustice, points
toward the struggle to probe the depth of meaning.

Because life presents us with ever-changing situations,
the meanings upon which we act are rarely static. Mildred,
age seventy-seven, states, "I thought by the time I got to
this age I would have all the answers and get everything
pinned down. But you just don't." We interpret experience and construe meaning throughout our life-span.

Sometimes the story of one event brings together the
threads of a life and symbolizes meaning as does
Mildred's: "We did a lot of community service. My
husband stood between the white community and the
black community. He was on the schoolboard when they
integrated the schools. When my husband died on a snowy
day, the yard was full of blacks, and they took off their
hats." Although her husband's death happened twenty-six
years before, its telling evoked tears. His efforts for justice,
bringing together the two communities, gave their lives
meaning.

But she hastened to add, "This sounds like I was kind of a do-gooder. I made the wrong decisions lots of times and fell on my face." For Mildred, this story encapsulates meanings because her husband's death was a turning point: She assumed responsibility for her own life and continued to struggle with issues of justice.

Humans also discover meanings as they connect personal meanings to meanings that are part of their cultures. Cultures provide shared symbols, a language, and expectations that form the context in which one learns. Persons who are part of a culture other than the dominant one encounter the power of community early in life. Chen, a Chinese youth whose mother does not speak English and forbids him to date his Anglo girlfriend, finds himself in the clash between two cultures. He struggles with the values of his Chinese family and his teenage friends. He makes and discovers meanings as he negotiates between two conflicting worlds.

We are most comfortable with the shared meanings of our communities of origin. Finding meaning in a culture different from our own is difficult. Meaning, however, can bridge cultures when people listen deeply to another's ways and risk honoring differences.

The meaning-making documented in the lives of contemporary people also occurred for biblical characters. Sarah, for instance, is introduced as barren: "Now, Sarai, Abram's wife, bore him no children" (Gen. 16:1). Her inability to conceive defined her identity. Renita Weems, a biblical scholar, states forcefully the meaning of this identity: "As the wife of Abram, who was a socially prominent and successful herdsman, Sarai was a wealthy woman in her community. As a Hebrew mistress, she was a woman of immense social and economic standing. But Sarai was barren. And in the culture in which Sarai lived, a woman's womb was her destiny."[5]

So when God promised Sarai that she would bear a child, even though she was past the age of childbearing, she laughed. This child would utterly change the meaning of her life. What else could she do but laugh!

Human beings do make and remake meaning. Travis reached his decision in the midst of conflicting experiences with the seminary and the army. The young boy at the mining accident was caught up in a life-and-death struggle, watching efforts to bring his father out of the mine. Mildred reflected on the years of stress her family faced as the schools were integrated. Chen adjudicated two conflicting worlds. Sarah learned to live as a mother. Experiences swirl about us. The values of our communities are omnipresent. Out of life experience, we derive meaning.

In order to connect this concept with your experience, draw your own temple of meaning. Include key events, relationships, and experiences that have shaped it. Discuss your drawing with a friend. Explain the meanings that are central for you.

Meaning Is Expressed as Story, Concept, or Image

Sometimes meaning is in the form of story, sometimes a concept, and sometimes at the edge of language, as image. Families tell stories at a death to express meanings. Travis constructed concepts in his written justification to explain his views about being a C.O. In contrast, Mildred's recollection of the day of her husband's death is rich with images and symbols—the whiteness of a "snowy day" and the dark skin of the people standing outside. Stories, concepts, and images flow back and forth together as people seek meaning.[6]

Story: This is a primary way we make and discover meaning. So, what is a story? Psychologist Dan McAdams observes that while almost everyone over the age of five can identify a story, controversy continues over a definition. Some define *story* as an event which evokes a change in a situation. For others, the focus is on a person who seeks to carry out an action and live with its consequences.[7]

Regardless of how we technically define *story*, we seem to know intuitively how a story should feel. There is a sense of events and people influencing each other. For example, when a couple on their fiftieth anniversary tells the story of their wedding day, the details foreshadow their children and their fifty years together. Their present remakes their past. They are actors in the narrative, causing events and reacting to the consequences. Events and people interact. As we tell stories, we weave events into meaning and communicate meanings to others.

Concept: Concepts are a more abstract way of defining meaning. They try to summarize our beliefs in a focused, defined phrase. Sometimes even when telling stories, we discover concepts. For example, when Chen was about to leave his girlfriend for a trip to China arranged by his family so he could learn the ways of his people, he shared his pain with a friend. In the midst of the story about where he would stay, for how long, and what he would be doing, he identified the cultural value of duty to family and tradition, and its conflict with the values of autonomy and individualism. He claimed the image of seeing with two sets of eyes: one set of the Chinese son and the other of the U.S. teenager. His insight was stated in a concept: The conflict results from living in two cultures.

Image: Images provide power for stories and concepts. Images are prelinguistic, coming in flashes of insight but not yet formed into a story or concept. Images are often richly sensory. Walter, for example, grew up working with his grandmother in the fertile soil of her garden. Even today, each spring as he spades the ground for planting, the smell of the earth brings memories of his grandmother flooding back, reminding him of who he is, and some of the values to which he tightly holds. Images and symbols evoke meanings powerfully. They occur at the connecting point between deep feelings and our ability to name experience.

Drawing on your own experience, perhaps during a time of crisis, express the meanings you made. Think of a story, concept, or image that helped you discover that meaning.

Meaning Is Theological

Central to being human is knowing that we are mortal. We live in the midst of paradox: We are finite, yet our actions influence the future. The struggle of living is knowing how to exist between finitude and hope in the future. The making and remaking of meanings, in their fullest and deepest dimensions, is therefore theological. Caught in the paradox, we ask ultimate questions about our destinies and about God.

When the walls of our temples of meaning tumble down or the floors give way to the ground of being, the temple must be reconstructed. Sharon Parks, a researcher in human development, tells us that "to be human is to dwell in faith, to dwell in one's meaning—one's conviction of the ultimate character of truth, of self, of world, of cosmos."[8] Many of us do not speak easily of these theological meanings. Yet the grounding values upon which we live are theological, defining for each of us what is good and lasting, and how we relate holistically to the cosmos.

After telling the story of her life, Mildred was asked, "So what is the meaning of life?"

She answered, "I guess the meaning comes through—it's the love."

To the same question, Travis said, "Hold onto your roots and the things that brought you where you are today, and hold onto 'em real tight." Both these meanings lead directly into theological affirmations of the nature of creation, of God, and of our relatedness to one another.

The boy who asked, "Why does He [God] sit back and let that happen?" is asking Job's questions about injustice, the existence of evil, and the power and goodness of God.

Madeleine L'Engle, who has written many volumes which explore living theological questions, notes in *The Summer of the Great Grandmother,* a story about the debilitation and death of her mother: "But I did feel, and passionately, that it wasn't fair of God to give us brains enough to ask the ultimate questions if He didn't intend to teach us the answers."[9] It is not that there are no answers. Rather, the answers flow from life experience. Because our life experiences take many turns, meanings we make along the way must be revised. Theology is a continuous process of interpreting our lives in relationship to ultimate questions—in relation to God. We struggle to discover truths on which we can stake our lives.

Expressing Meaning
Through Identity and Vocation

Wilfred Cantwell Smith, historian of religion, described the process of discovering and making meaning with this quip: "Crocodiles have no difficulty in being crocodiles." In contrast, to be "human does require special effort; or special thought; or special grace." We can fail to be human, "fail properly to recognize the authentic humanity of one's neighbor, can treat other men and women as if they were less than human."[10] Crocodiles just do what they were born to do—swim beneath the surface looking for prey to fulfill hunger. We human beings, on the other hand, choose how to live and how to affect the world.

Each day as we awake, we endeavor to make sense of the world. Sometimes we look in the mirror, see our aging faces, and grieve for lost opportunities. Sometimes we look at children and see our possibilities. Sometimes we stand with those like us, facing pain and oppression. Sometimes we are terrorized by what waits before us. Sometimes we celebrate gifts given to us by those who love us and sponsor us into the future. Sometimes we walk through routine days, repeating what we always do and encountering few questions.

Humans have an innate need to express meanings. Speaking of her Sunday school class, one middle-aged woman said, "I don't feel right if I miss it. I like the interaction. You have to define in your own mind your own faith before you can say it." The interaction with these people helps that woman know what she has discovered and allows her to test her meanings. For some, the expression of meaning is found through faithful attendance at worship. Sitting in the pew on Sunday morning is a concrete way to witness, to hear the stories, and to dwell on the symbols that are important for their lives. For others, it may come in efforts for justice. Working together in a community organization to rehabilitate houses is a way to express one's faith. Our choices of activity, as well as our statements of belief, are expressions of our meanings.

The Search for Identity and Vocation

Who am I? What am I to do? My life experience—the culture, the family, the place, the events, the relationships—forms my understanding of my identity and of the way I will live out that identity in vocation.

Identity forms as we answer the question, "Who am I in relation to others, to creation, and to God?" In many cultures rituals have developed around the issues of identity. Naming ceremonies, for instance, help us to know both our personal and our public identities. In some traditions, the naming of a creature or person gave one power over it. The changing of the names of Abram and Sarai to Abraham and Sarah made concrete their changed relationship to Yahweh: "No longer shall your name be Abram, but your name shall be Abraham; for I have made you the ancestor of a multitude of nations" (Gen. 17:5). The name change indicated God's relationship with Abraham's future and the family to which Abraham now belonged. Similarly, the search for a medical diagnosis—a name to put on one's malaise—grows out of the need to know an illness and thus gain power over it.

Charles was given his grandfather's name. As patriarch of the family, the grandfather was a hero who had triumphed over illness and poverty. When the grandfather died, several of his treasured possessions were given to his grandson. Charles told the story: "The gift of his watch and the knife were special. I was now Charles. I was the only one with his name. I was expected to be a leader." Charles gained a fuller identity.

Ethnicity is another powerful example of identity. Malcolm tells of a trip with his youngest son. The events around the march on Birmingham led by Martin Luther King, Jr., were to be reenacted. Malcolm knew that there his son could experience the power of his African American heritage, could come to know himself, and would learn of the struggle for justice and human rights. As the son and father prepared to march, the father told his son the story of his own life and that of his people. The son learned about his own identity.

Identity is always defined in relationship to the people and communities whose meanings nurture us. Dan McAdams has discovered that "how the whole person understands his or her 'wholeness' " is a central issue. Each of us weaves a life story that is "a joint product of person and environment. In a sense the two write the story together."[11] As we weave the life story, we seek a wholeness which provides unity and purpose.

Vocation is a response to our striving for wholeness. We need to find a way to be fully all that we can be and are called to be: loving, in relationship, contributing to the world in interdependent ways. Aspects of our living always fall short of that goal. We hurt those we love. We participate in oppressive systems. We fail to act in accord with values. Yet, we also struggle to live up to our calling. Mildred, for example, discovered that her husband's stand for social justice provided a frame of reference for her as she defined her own vocation. She seems to enjoy being a "do-gooder."

Vocation is also the issue for Adrienne, a middle-aged woman who speaks of her struggle to fulfill her commitment to God. After teaching in public school for many years, she completed a doctorate and moved into university teaching. She relished this new career. However, questions that students and friends kept raising called her to reassess where she could best serve. They saw her as willing to share in ultimate questions. Adrienne responded by exploring ministry as a career. She talked with her pastor and friends at church and school. She entered her denomination's candidacy program for ordination and visited theological seminaries. After the exploration, she decided to remain in teaching and moved to a liberal arts college where she could share faith issues in the classroom. After successfully negotiating a doctorate and embarking on a career, she had again to explore her choice.

James Fowler, a faith-development researcher, defines vocation as "the response a person makes with his or her total self to the address of God and to the calling to partnership."[12] It is an orchestration that blends all of one's life—leisure, relationships, work, private life, public life, and the resources we steward—to embody one's meanings. Vocation includes both our achievements (what we have done) and our being (the meanings that we stand for through our lives). Through identity and vocation, our meanings are expressed.

Responding to the Search for Identity and Vocation

We all deal with the search for identity and vocation in very personal ways. Some persons avoid the search by failing to ask questions. Often they are stalled by past meanings given to them by authorities. Their temples are constructed with prefabricated walls, which may not be securely fastened at the corners. Others settle for one meaning in one part of their lives—for example, Sunday morning—and live other meanings in other parts, as at work. They thus separate their lives. Their temple consists of several small buildings with no secure passages between them. Still others seek to integrate their lives and meanings, recognizing that ambiguity and dissonance continue to be present. Their temples are whole, but still under construction, with the final form and decoration still in doubt. Living in the midst of the construction project brings anxiety as well as excitement and intensity to life.

All of us respond to the meanings that have emerged out of our life experience. They profoundly affect the way we live. Yet, the ways we express meaning are different for different people. For some, the living of daily life is sufficient. Richard, a retired university professor, indicated that he spent little time struggling with questions of meaning: "You live life. If my life can't speak it, then I can't say it." Richard is comfortable with the tacit meanings lived through his identity and vocation. Others share their meanings regularly. Adrienne learned that she could not teach English without engaging in conversations about meanings.

Whether or not we spend much time in conversation, our lives reflect our meanings. Periodically, we face limits to meaning. Crises upset life. Change brings new options. We then seek, with the aid of others, to restore or transform the patterns out of which we live. When taking life for granted is challenged, all of us reflect and remake meanings.

Meaning and Its Functions

Meaning is an interpretation of life experience. Chen, for example, understood the trip to China as his parents' attempt to control his values. When he realized their motivation, he also came to see that he too is Chinese, even as he is part of U.S. culture. He interprets his experience in light of the ambiguity and dissonance of two sets of cultural values.

Functions of Meaning

Philosopher Roy D'Andrade lists four functions of meaning: to re-present, to construct, to evoke, or to direct.[13] Each of these functions clarifies the dynamics of meaning-making and meaning discovery.

First, meaning functions to *re-present* reality. Meaning names an aspect of reality. For example, knowing the name for the pains we feel often relieves anxiety and gives us direction for living; knowing that we have arthritis in a shoulder can provide the information needed to help us decide how to act. Meaning re-presents knowledge when it corresponds with observed data.

Second, meaning *constructs* when it provides content for social agreements. Each cultural group has a set of values. Discovering shared meanings or listening intently to the meanings of others is necessary to enable us to interact appropriately. For example, profound changes have taken place in Eastern Europe. Georg, a teacher in what was East Germany, maintains that people there are coming to understand freedom more fully. They are learning the value of freedom of choice. However, he also hopes that his people will not lose another meaning of freedom—that is, freedom from want. In the past, his society has honored the importance of providing work and welfare to each person. Georg wants freedom to include both individual initiative and corporate responsibility. His people are constructing meanings.

Third, meaning *evokes* as it arouses affective responses. For example, when United Methodist annual conferences begin by singing "And Are We Yet Alive?" the participants are connected to values shared by the group. A song like "This Land Is Your Land" or "We Shall Overcome" evokes the feelings one had while demonstrating on the grounds of the Washington Monument. Meaning can arouse intense and shared feelings.

Finally, meaning *directs*. Meaning leads to action on the part of an individual or community. For example, a person who discovers that she is called to work with others to build community will seek ways to live out that commitment through her career in social work. Meaning helps us name the world, construct values, feel, and make choices.

We Always Remake Meanings

As we come to know and live our meanings—as we are recognizing the temples of meaning in which we dwell—the construction remains tentative. A narrative cannot be the same twice; its retelling is a new event. Those who speak to more than one group or congregation can attest to this fact. The same speech or sermon, even read from a manuscript, takes on new meanings each time. The people are different; the time is different. What we learn between speeches or sermons changes the way the message is spoken.

The meanings that shape a story may be reshaped in the telling. As a family talks at the funeral of Aunt Sarah, niece Darlene begins to see that her teenage perceptions did not recognize the woman's yearning for greater challenges and fulfillment. As an adult, Darlene remakes her memories of Sarah. She realizes how hungry Sarah was for adventure and joy. The story has new meaning, and Darlene understands herself differently in light of it. She comes to more acceptance of her own hunger for adventure and joy as constitutive of her family heritage and its heroic women.

The process of meaning-making and remaking is a muddle. Often our meanings are ambiguous. Each telling of our story is a rehearsal, practicing meanings. Some meanings endure through time; others are destroyed. After Hiroshima, for example, we all learned that no place is absolutely safe. In the midst of the muddle, we offer preliminary hunches and come to moments of resolution.

As a couple faces a decision about whether to accept a new job and move to a new community, they talk together about who they are and to what their vocations call them. In the midst of the discussion, they reach a moment of resolution when they decide for or against moving. Whichever decision is reached, the resolution will again be questioned and adjusted in the future. Laura, telling of a move to another state forced by the termination of her husband's job, found that she had lost a great deal.

"What's really important?" she asked. "The job, relationships, family. The job has been too important to me. You need other people outside your family circle. Your happiness isn't just in yourself. It's in your relationships." Losing those close relationships as a result of the move brought about a new set of meanings for Laura.

Recall a time when, like Darlene or Laura, you remade a meaning. Note some of the feelings, values, or commitments that changed for you.

Sometimes we remake meanings mutually, in conversation. We talk meanings out. We find a friend or spouse who will listen as we try to understand. Occasionally, more intentional settings—counseling, grief groups, or Sunday school classes—prove beneficial. Remaking in community lets us express and even test our meanings. In turn, as we hear others express their meanings, we find ourselves challenged. At other times, meaning is remade through introspection and reflection. The process of remaking meanings continues.

In the meaning system of the young boy who was asking why God let the mine disaster happen, a caring God with great power was in control. The disaster, however, called that meaning into question. How could a loving God let his father die? When our temples of meaning appear inadequate to explain our life experiences, we face meaninglessness. Meanings must bear the test of lived experience. Inadequate meanings make us feel anxious and can misdirect our energies.

Pain accompanies times when meaning is challenged. Our temple may crumble under stress; we feel homeless, at the mercy of the elements. Sharon Parks describes these times with the metaphor of shipwreck:

> To undergo shipwreck is to be threatened in a most total and primary way. Shipwreck is the coming apart of what has served as shelter and protection and has held and carried one where one wanted to go—the collapse of a structure that once promised trustworthiness. Likewise, when we undergo the shipwreck of meaning at the level of faith, we feel threatened at the very core of our existence.[14]

The human need to make, remake, and discover meaning undergirds all of who we are and what we do.

In summary, all human beings seek meanings for their lives. We dwell in meanings which arise from our encounter with life. We find ourselves expressing and reformulating these meanings as we remember and tell our stories. Sometimes meaning is expressed in concepts. At other times, meaning is known through images and is more affective than rational. Meaning pushed to ultimate questions is theological, speaking of the nature of God and of our calling as God's creatures. We can live in the face of death because our lives have meaning. Meaning provides hope. And finally, our lives—our vocations and identities—are the fruits of meaning.

CHAPTER TWO

SEEING WITH NEW EYES

Making and Discovering Meaning

Every day, we struggle to discover meaning and make sense of our experiences. Chen searched for his *identity* among his people and his friends in the United States. Adrienne reassessed her *vocation* to find ways to fulfill her commitment to God. The injustices and crises of life raise questions such as those of the young boy whose father died in the mine. The search for meaning is a natural human process. In this chapter, writing as educators, we explore one side of faith—faith as a *human* meaning-perspective. In chapter 3, we move to theology, to affirm grace as the ground of meaning and faith as a gift of God.

The Human Process of Meaning

Our call to make and discover meaning is illustrated every day. A chaplain told of an older woman from a wealthy family, who one Friday was moved from her home to a care institution. She arrived during the shift change, and because of the hour, her paperwork was misplaced until Monday morning. During the weekend, she explored the facility, met people, and enjoyed the meals. On Monday, the staff members were horrified when they discovered that no one had followed up on her "case." In their view, it was a case of gross negligence.

However, upon entering her room, they learned that her view was quite different. She remarked, "What a wonderful place! No one bothered me all weekend. I did what I wanted."

Why the discrepancy between the view of the staff and that of the woman? Which is true? Meanings are always made in the context of our experiences, our histories, our commitments, and the cultures in which we live. The staff's perspective was defined by responsibility and care. Neither had been exercised in this situation. The woman had been "lost," the "case" mishandled. Had something serious happened to her, they would have been liable. Their lawyers were horrified.

From the woman's perspective, she had always been alone and self-reliant. Raised in an environment of absent parents, she had learned to play by herself and take care of herself. Following her husband's death twenty-five years before, those early patterns had been reinforced. In fact, the day she was moved to the center, she most feared losing her independence. The first weekend confirmed that she could survive in her new home, because the structures she counted on were reinforced. Unfortunately, the dismay exhibited by the staff reinstituted her worry. She wanted her independence.

We Perceive Meanings in Context

Meanings are embedded in the structures of our cultures, the world itself, and our personal experiences. These structures of meaning are exhibited by John "Fire" Lame Deer as he describes differences between his people (the Sioux) and Anglo American culture:

But I'm an Indian. I think about ordinary, common things, like this pot [in which I am cooking]. The bubbling water comes from the rain cloud. It represents the sky. The fire comes from the sun which warms all of us—men, animals, trees. The meat stands for the four-legged creatures, our animal brothers, who gave of themselves so we should live. The steam is living breath. It was water; now it goes up to the sky, becomes a cloud again. These things are sacred.[1]

In the Sioux way of perceiving, common things have spiritual dimensions: "We see in the world around us many symbols that teach us the meaning of life. We have a saying that the white man sees so little, he must see with only one eye."[2]

Lame Deer observes that meaning is dependent upon what we see, to what we attend. Anyone who has been caught between two cultures knows the difficulty of adjudicating the expectations of each. Meanings, even our theological meanings, are framed within our personal histories; and these are set within structures given by our cultures. Moreover, both personal and cultural meanings depend upon limits (boundaries) present in our worlds. But while these limits are real, even they are affected by our perspectives (our temples of meaning). As Lame Deer says to his Anglo listeners, "We see a lot that you no longer notice. You could notice if you wanted to, but you are usually too busy."[3] We all live in a world of images, concepts, and stories. We draw on these as we attempt to understand and communicate with others.

Often, as Lame Deer says, "We need no more than a hint to give us meaning."[4] Much of the time, we live in an orderly world, drawing on past clues to replicate meanings as we walk through life. When these ordinary clues do not work, the process of meaning-making and discovery is made apparent.

We are unable to take in all the aspects of our experience, so we choose which portions we will notice. This process is described as perception. We review new experiences by drawing "upon our past knowledge to make interpretations that help us choose the dimensions of a new experience to which we will attend."[5] Perception is unique; it depends upon our unique experiences and prior learnings. Two persons will perceive the same event differently. How many times have you left a meeting, and then talked at length with another participant, checking your perceptions of what happened? Each of us makes different choices, interpreting that slice of experience in our own way—as a result of our past, the experience itself, and the commitments we hold.

However, personal meanings are validated and reinterpreted in community. As a family gathers for a funeral, they tell stories of how Aunt Sarah lived. These stories reinforce and reinterpret each other, suggesting dimensions of who she was. Darlene, the niece, tells how much fun she had as a teenager on a swimming expedition, as they giggled over the flirtatious young man who sold them gasoline. That story gains more dimensions when a sister tells of how Sarah made Rome fun on a hot and humid day, even with a traffic jam and a stalled bus. Together, the family builds a picture of a woman brimming with energy and life, who helped people enjoy moments to their fullest. We remake our personal meanings communally.

The community in which we live defines, to a great extent, what we will perceive. Many slave owners avoided their sin by perceiving their African American laborers as childish and happy. The slaves' nobility, grief, and inner strength went unnoticed. The culture limited the perception of the slave owners. Similarly, during the Cold War, many Americans perceived Russians as cold, uncaring

automatons. With glasnost, we have rediscovered the
Russian people as fully human. Our cultures and
communities influence what we will notice and, therefore,
how we will make meaning.

This communal dimension means that all of us are
socialized. The process of making, remaking, and
discovering meaning is learned. Our neighborhoods teach
us much about meanings. For instance, the child who lives
in the housing project learns "hard" lessons from that
context. As Alex Kotlowitz documents, children in the
projects face mortality early. One young boy commented
to a friend after a funeral, "We're gonna die one way or
the other, by killing or plain out. I just wanna die plain
out." His friend nodded. "Me too."[6] That interchange
illustrates profound understandings which the boys
developed as they interpreted the experience of a friend's
death. The meaning was made communally, although it
stemmed from very personal perceptions. While meaning-making occurs naturally, meanings are shaped and
reshaped (learned) within communities.

Meaning and Faith

Meanings are both shaped by culture and created by us.
Culture shapes our meanings; we live in the perspectives
of the worlds we are "given." This is socialization.
However, we also create meanings as we seek to integrate
the new into our past frames of reference. Living in the
twentieth century means living in the midst of the
challenge to traditional authority structures which seem
inadequate to address the rapidity of change. We know
that our interpretations are fallible and often culturally
dependent. We need to be in a constant process of
reflection and dialogue—testing, refining, reshaping.

Mezirow describes the process of meaning-making,

drawing on two concepts: meaning-perspective and meaning-scheme. A meaning-perspective is the tacit "structure of assumptions" through which one perceives, integrates, and incorporates new experience; meaning-perspectives focus and limit our meanings. The meaning-scheme is the conscious content we use to express our meanings. Metaphorically, meaning-perspectives are the foundations of our temples of meaning; meaning-schemes are the ways the rooms are painted and arranged.

"A meaning-perspective is a habitual set of expectations which constitutes an orienting frame of reference."[7] A meaning-perspective is the tacit deep structure (frame of reference) within each of us, through which all experience passes; it is foundational. Meaning-perspectives organize and shape our experiences. For example, Lame Deer's Sioux way was a meaning-perspective. Lame Deer contrasted his frame of reference with that of the "white man." His world *expected* the spiritual. The Sioux meaning-perspective allowed that any experience could open up the spiritual meaning of life. In contrast, Lame Deer thought that the white man saw only one dimension because the public world in the United States was "scientific." The U.S. meaning-perspective tends to expect ordinary and observable meanings from experience.

Meaning-perspectives, frames of reference, are the structures through which experience is focused. They thus limit what we expect and what we see. Simon, a friend from the Pacific Islands, describes the practice of healing in his culture. While "Western" medical procedures are important to diagnosis and cure, traditional patterns of healing which involve spirit discernment and exorcism are also practiced by some "medically trained" doctors. His argument is that the meaning-perspective of his culture is open to more than "Western" medicine. His world expects more.

In fact, he explains that Western medicine itself is trying to incorporate holistic healing, involving body, emotions, mind, and spirit. The traditional meaning-perspective of his culture expected illness and healing to be spiritual; the Western system expects illness and healing to be scientific. The meaning-perspectives that organize medicine in both cultures are tacit structures which guide understandings of healing, filtering experiences, and controlling meanings.

The process of filtering experiences and categorizing them into accepted patterns is usually unconscious. However, in moments of crisis, our meaning-perspectives can be under considerable pressure as their ability to provide meaningful frames of reference for experience is challenged. The meaning-perspective that informed many conservative leaders in the Soviet Union in the summer of 1991 was profoundly challenged as they discovered that people no longer were willing to let military might dictate political change. The people had breathed a new spirit of change and freedom that had reshaped their meaning-perspectives. Their meaning-perspectives now included the tacit conviction of the people's power.

Experiences are always filtered through the deep ground of our meaning-perspectives. Meaning is dependent upon interpreting fresh experience in continuity with the past. When this fails, a new perspective is needed.

Cut out a picture from a magazine. Using another piece of paper, frame the picture in different ways. Tell a story about each view. Note how the stories change as the perspective used to filter the picture changes.

Meaning-schemes, on the other hand, are the more conscious beliefs and positions we hold. They are felt passionately but are more fluid, changing with argument and conversation:

> A *meaning scheme is the particular knowledge, beliefs, value judgments, and feelings that become articulated in an experience.* . . . A meaning scheme may pertain to how to do something (instrumental learning), how to understand what others mean (communicative learning), or how to understand oneself.[8]

Two friends may passionately hold differing positions about a decision, yet the frame of reference called *friendship* is not in jeopardy. In the midst of an argument, with all its emotions and ambiguities, one friend may change an opinion or belief. The meaning-scheme (the belief or opinion) is shifted.

In contrast to meaning-perspectives, meaning-schemes are the *conscious* beliefs, judgments, and feelings which we use as we communicate with others. For example, a scientifically trained doctor visiting a colleague in the Pacific Islands may learn a new procedure for dealing with a sick person, drawn from the work of the traditional medicine man, but the doctor does not shift her basic meaning-perspective of scientific medicine. In turn, a medicine man may learn a new procedure for cure without changing a meaning-perspective based on a spiritual reading of healing. The meaning-scheme is the content (the new procedure learned); the meaning-perspective is the organizing filter (scientific or spiritual healing).

Meaning-schemes provide the content through which we communicate our beliefs and commitments. Meaning-perspectives provide the organizing frame within which the content is expressed. As we encounter a culture significantly different from our own, we may accept new ideas, knowledge, and feelings without substantially shifting the tacit structure by which we organize meaning.

Racism is an example of the relationship between meaning-perspective and meaning-scheme. A person raised in a racist culture may have learned certain rules by which people are judged and by which society is organized. Those meaning-perspectives limit and define the way others are seen. Because of political pressure, such a person may change the way he or she interacts with someone of another race, but still organize reality in such a way that the other is seen as inferior. Meaning-perspectives are especially powerful because they are tacit and foundational. Another person may change beliefs about another race because of argument or political necessity, but it is more difficult for the orienting frame of reference to shift. Long after one accepts the principle of equality based on race or gender, one still may be telling jokes that violate the principles one espouses. The jokes reflect the meaning-perspective. They touch deeply into the orienting structure.

Both meaning-schemes (content) and meaning-perspectives (structure) are essential to the process of meaning-making. Their relationship to each other is dynamic. Many changes in beliefs will affect the way a perspective can be organized. A fundamental shift in perspective will transform the meanings of beliefs. To engage another person's meanings is to deal with both meaning-schemes and meaning-perspectives.

Meaning-perspectives provide the foundational structures we use to define life, expectations, and ourselves. When they are challenged, we risk meaninglessness and social disruption; our temples crumble. Meaning-perspectives are parallel to what recent conversation in social science and religious education calls faith.[9] In this literature, faith is a structure of meaning—the structure through which we order our world on the basis of convictions about trust, expectation, and value. *Faith*, then, is a system of convictions which defines for us what is of value, good, and real. Used this way, the word *faith* is the same as a meaning-perspective.

A faith grows from basic experiences of trust and fidelity in childhood. Moreover, it is generated by the very language we use. When we learn the meanings of certain words, we already assume a discourse of trust. "Chair" is always supposed to be an object to sit on.[10] Our faiths, our meaning-perspectives, form as we learn and participate in our culture. They are shaped both by *cultural patterns* acquired through daily life with a people—living in families and relationships, using a particular language, following expected canons of behavior—and by *personal patterns* that come from our own experience.

Making meaning is a venture of faith. We trust our points of view. We rely on our meaning-perspectives to interpret our experiences.

Making and Discovering Meaning

Lame Deer is correct: Usually we need no more than a hint to give us meaning, because we live in a world shaped by our cultures and our personal histories. Often meaning-making happens intuitively. Past experiences of naming and arranging reality form the riverbanks through which current events stream. We possess fixed, settled perspectives through which life is experienced and interpreted. Thus meaning seems to happen effortlessly. However, there are occasions when a person's experiences cannot be interpreted within familiar frameworks. Events overflow the riverbanks and change the landscape. On these occasions, we are called to enlarge or reshape the perspectives on which we rely. New river channels must be dredged.

The Ways Meanings Function

There are at least three ways we make and discover meaning: We remember, we reconstruct, and we are transformed. Much of the time, we act spontaneously. We *remember*. Information is taken in and filtered through our perception. We see a stop sign as we approach an intersection, and we automatically brake. Much of the time, we "go with the flow"; experiences fit within our frames of reference. Through much of daily life, we remember how to act. A baby cries; we pick the child up and check for a wet diaper. A friend cries; we reach out in support, asking what is wrong.

However, at other times we are called to reflect upon experience and information, and either fit it within our perspectives or remake our perspectives. The two remaining ways of making meaning progressively take more energy and are more threatening to the patterns by which we live daily life: (1) we reconstruct meanings; and (2) our perspectives are transformed. Meeting these challenges, we draw on images, stories, and concepts (our meaning-schemes).

Sometimes we must reconstruct meanings. Old patterns are no longer effective. For example, when we drive a friend's car, many of the devices are in new places. If we learned to dim the headlights with a button under our left foot, we are in trouble if the car does not have such a button. No amount of remembering will help. Jack drove an unfamiliar car for three hours with the bright lights on because he did not know that the switch was on the turn-signal. After reconstructing the possibility that a switch or button could be elsewhere, a meaning emerges that could be used in future situations.

Or when we meet a friend we have not seen for several years, we may begin to talk as if we had never been separated, but soon we learn of profound changes in the friend's life (a divorce, the death of a parent, a new career). We discover that we need to reconstruct the basic way we respond to our friend. Our action is still related to past actions, but our past meanings are changed by new circumstances.

Finally, we all have experiences which shatter our meaning-perspectives. Relocation, loss of a job, divorce, injustice, illness—any of these can stimulate the transforming. Profound changes occur. The very patterns which preserved stability and order are themselves shattered. The risk of chaos and meaninglessness are real possibilities unless we can reestablish a perspective out of which meaning is made. A significant illness is a powerful example. For the person who is ill, accepted patterns of behavior may no longer be trusted, no longer function effectively.

Jim, a sportswriter, had a heart attack. For twenty years, he had lived a hard-driving life of long hours and road trips. His illness meant that he had to reassess his schedule and its stresses. As he sought to reintegrate himself, he also discovered the patterns by which he had related to his family, confessing that he had missed his oldest child's years at home. Jim's religious faith became a profound resource as his temple of meaning was transformed. "Grace" found him. His illness was a call to know what it means to be a child of God and live with an identity not totally dependent upon achievements. Transformation took place in the way he looked at himself, his job, and his family.

He is still learning to live with new challenges, but he is clearly aware of processing experience anew: "Change is still in process. I haven't yet learned to stop smoking. But my schedule is very different. I even see my kids in sports, rather than other people's kids. I'm learning a little of what God wants of me."

Distortions in Meaning-making

In the process of filtering experiences through accepted patterns, and remembering, reconstructing, or transforming, there is a possibility of distortion. As a result of fear and the threat of chaos, we can resist change by holding onto older patterns. An example may be those who failed to listen to the new word that Jesus brought.

The Gospel of Mark records that people resisted transformation. The Gospel writer focused on Jesus' increasing frustration with the blindness of the religious leaders. Their expectations about the kingdom of God distorted their view of Jesus and blinded them to the gift of God's reign and realm emerging in actions of healing, forgiveness, and justice all around them. Jesus wept over Jerusalem because of the unwillingness of people to be transformed. He also challenged the faithlessness of his disciples. Blinded by their own search for glory, they jockeyed for position in his kingdom.[11] Their meaning-perspectives limited their understanding of Jesus' message and identity.

Our perceptions of reality can be distorted and therefore our judgments may be flawed. Sometimes we examine life with a mote in our eye. Our perceptions seldom, if ever, correspond totally with the truth. A poem by R. D. Laing illustrates that myopia:

> The range of what we think and do
> is limited by what we fail to notice.
> And because we fail to notice
> there is little we can do
> to change
> until we notice
> how failing to notice
> shapes our thoughts and deeds.[12]

Meaning is a result of the structures of the world in which we find ourselves; meaning emerges from the communities that nurture and socialize us; meaning is affected by our capacities for learning; and meaning is shaped by how we handle past experiences. Much of the time, we live automatically, using past meanings to filter and shape new experiences. Yet, when experiences do not fit, we reconstruct meanings, or our meaning-perspectives are transformed.

Meaning and Education

Education involves both socialization (faith formation), by which the basic cultural patterns of a people are appropriated, and faith transformation, where, through dialogue and reflection, our meaning-perspectives are reshaped. When education functions as socialization, it transmits the patterns of meaning embodied in the events, experiences, personalities, rituals, and symbols of our heritage. However, the experiences of individuals and groups, as well as cross-cultural interaction, challenge these accepted meaning-perspectives and reveal new possibilities. When we experience such challenges, education needs to be about faith transformation.

Faith and meaning-making are common to all humanity. However, the diversities of peoples across both time and space can no longer be ignored. Meaning-making happens within particular historical, political, economic, and cultural circumstances. Each culture has a depth, richness, and power which creates unique meanings, and education and religion must affirm this diversity. Nevertheless, we are able to share our meanings and seek to build life together. We must learn that meanings are not to be imposed on people; they are negotiated among people. Our faith leads us to affirm that grace is the ground of meaning-making—meaning is present in the cosmos. The description of human faith now needs to be expanded. That is the task of chapter 3.

CHAPTER THREE

AMAZING GRACE

Faith and Religion

The last ten days had been difficult. The participants on the mission trip—ten students, a chaplain, two clergy, and two faculty members from a U.S. college—had struggled to communicate in Spanish. Without their translators, they would have been lost. They had also struggled physically as they built a school in the humidity of the Central American mountains. But most of all, they had struggled to fathom the experience of working side by side with people who seemed to have so few possessions, but possessed such greatness of spirit.

Although these people from the U.S. would be returning to their studies and careers, they felt vulnerable. Their meaning-perspectives had been challenged. *Generous, open, connected, oppressed,* and *faithful* were words they used to describe the people they had come to know as they laughed and worked together through broken Spanish and English. *Possessions, individuality, enthusiastic,* and *faithful* were words that became increasingly powerful in their understanding of themselves. They knew that new feelings and meanings were emerging. The villagers had graced them with the love of family. Even the personal changes they would face when they returned home would be set in this context of grace. Hours of talking had helped them begin to make sense of the experience, but they knew that more conversation and support would be needed.[1]

Gregory described their last night in Central America and how it had graciously empowered their search for meaning:

> We walked along a mud path next to the city dump, an area known as the misery beltway. Humberto and Maria had built their lean-to shelter with sheets of blue plastic and chunks of rotting plywood dragged out of the trash. They wore cast-off clothing; they ate refuse prepared and served in plastic and aluminum ware others had spurned. They washed clothes, bathed in, and drank from the glittering but polluted river down the hill. A slat-thin dog with dazed yellow eyes guarded the path to their hut. Images of despair, degradation, and death silenced our voices and stilled the whir and click of our cameras. Maria would not talk to us, but she made coffee with her last beans, enough for one serving in a broken cup. We were stunned. We ached and wept in our efforts to absorb the meaning of her fabulous gift. As each of us took the cup, the coffee became the wine of the Eucharist.

The guests and the villagers had touched one another. The guests learned much about life and friendship, hope and despair. Like Cleopas and a friend on the road to Emmaus, these visitors saw the risen one, God's incarnation, in the villagers and in this simple but unexpected celebration. They saw the Christ image reflected in the liquid in the cracked cup, in the beams of light rising from the ruined river, in Maria's averted glances, in Humberto's shame-masking smile, and in the villagers' courage. They knew the hospitality of Christ as Maria gave all that she possessed. Thanks to God was the only appropriate response. Indeed, "hearts burned" as they encountered the Holy One.

The visitors had come from a culture of plenty, where sharing a cup of coffee was an expected ritual, easy to fulfill. They trusted in hospitality. Here, where possessions were precious, they learned that hospitality and love were still to be trusted, but were much more costly.

Six months later, many of those on the mission trip were still integrating their learnings into daily living. Their vulnerability showed as they talked with friends and families, with church groups, and in the campus ministry. Some had priorities shifted, seeing study and careers in new light. Some made mutual commitments with those in Central America, together planning future projects and visits. Some continued in old ways, with a tug of guilt that things should be different. The hospitality and grace their hosts had offered provided hope as they struggled for meaning.

Gregory told us about how his view of the church had changed. In his local congregation, during communion, the pastor "feeds" each parishioner the bread and wine. However, the experience in Central America was that everyone shared, out of their lives together. The "bread" and "wine" passed among the participants was a family meal.

"Each way seems to communicate a different view of the church," he said. "My local church sees ministry as something the pastor does to or for us. On the trip, we learned something different. We were the people of God, sharing in ministry to one another. I don't know if my church can understand ministry that way."

New experiences either take root within or challenge the basic perspectives of faith through which we live. Faith is a meaning-perspective, but faith is more. Faith is a gracious gift of God. Discovering meaning rests on trust in our experiences, in others, and in grace that surprisingly encounters us. Faith as gift is the subject of this chapter. Faith funds religion.

In religions, meanings are gathered into stories, concepts (doctrines), and images (symbols), which provide direction for living. Religions themselves are systems of meaning, with a past (a tradition) and a trajectory into the future (a vision). Sociologist and priest Andrew Greeley describes the connection of grace and religion:

> *Religion becomes a communal event when a person is able to link his own grace experience with the overarching experience of his religious tradition* (or a religious tradition), that is to say, when he perceives a link between his experience of grace and the tradition's experience of grace when he becomes aware that there is a correspondence or a correlation between the resonating picture or story in his imagination and the story passed on by his religious heritage.[2]

When our meaning-perspectives and those of a religion resonate harmoniously, we dwell with vitality in a community of faith.

Grace as Ground of Meaning

The visitors to Central America encountered grace with the people they went to help. Meaning-perspectives by which they had lived were profoundly challenged. Some of the visitors were renewed. Others had difficulty reintegrating into jobs and families. Some have since "fallen away" from the commitments they made. Yet, all were touched by the grace found in the Central American mountains.

The power of grace is seen both in the order of life and

in responses to chaos. Jennifer, a five-year-old, recently attended the funeral of her grandfather.

After the service, she asked her aunt, "Aunt Ellen, how will Mark [her six-month-old brother] ever know about Grandpa?"

Ellen told her, "You'll have to tell him stories and show him pictures."

Two days later, Jennifer was sitting by Mark, telling him stories of her grandfather. It was not easy for her. She felt the pain of loss. Responding to grace, she came to know the order of life: With death is loss; with birth, new life. In fact, Ellen remarked that watching Jennifer ministered to her. Jennifer helped her see hope beyond the loss.

Grace also comes in the midst of chaos. On another day, Jennifer shouted at her aunt, "God doesn't care!"

When Ellen asked, "Why do you say that?" Jennifer responded, "I prayed that God would let me talk to Grandpa just one more time. And God doesn't let me. If I could talk to Grandpa, everything would be okay."

Grace in Chaos and Order

The world is not always trustworthy. People we count on—parents, spouses, children, employers, friends—let us down. Death and divorce end relationships. We sometimes violate old commitments as we live up to new expectations. Institutions to which we have devoted our lives close, and we lose jobs and benefits. Neighborhoods deteriorate and people are forced to live in the midst of violence. All of us face finitude, illness, and aging. Life is lived in the ambiguous and precarious balance between meanings that remain and are renewed, *and* structures that deteriorate. We live between order and chaos, never quite sure which is more powerful.

Theologian Belden Lane tells of his mother's diagnosis

of cancer, of her wasting body, and of his pain at being powerless to do anything for her. He admits:

> Difficult as it was, at first, to discern grace in the grotesque [the diagnosis], it has been even more difficult to discover grace in the prolonged redundancy of ordinariness [her slow deterioration]. How can I adjust to life's untheatrical regularity when I've been prepared for grand opera and dark tragedy. . . . It's the disconsolation of the ordinary that I've found most difficult to accept.[3]

All his life, he was being prepared to deal with catastrophe, learning to do battle with powers and principalities from which special grace could rescue him with "flair" and "boldness." When we think of grace, we usually think of the miraculous drama, the saving and healing that rescues us from chaos. A friend avoids harm in a tragic accident; we say, "You escaped by the grace of God." When we see people triumph over major physical and mental challenges, we see grace in their survival. The Christian tradition calls this "special grace."

Yet Lane discloses another grace. The experience of watching his mother die is teaching him something new: To remake his meanings by affirming common grace, the ordinary grace that "falls upon the just and unjust alike" through the order of daily life. "Life is more than a matter of breathless contention, triumphing over obstacles, denying the monsters of our own feelings."[4] There is a "quiet acceptance of life's rhythms." That is also grace.

Identify a common grace and/or a special grace you have experienced in your own life. What examples of either can you draw from remembered novels or stories?

John Wesley, the founder of Methodism, spoke of both common and special grace.[5] Wesley's term for common grace is *prevenient grace*—the gift of life itself. Prevenient grace sustains and nurtures us, and teaches us how to help or hinder life. Special grace is the dramatic rescue that turns us from sin and strengthens us to face tragedies. Wesley called it justifying grace (or salvation). Yet, in addition, Wesley spoke of a third kind of grace—sanctifying grace—the grace of love, which increasingly teaches us to care for life and others.

As our meanings are challenged, we turn to the sources that have sustained us. Sometimes we find order restored; at other times we are sent on a journey into our experiences, traditions, and friendships, to seek new options. The descriptions of grace by both Lane and Wesley clarify the way we risk change. Structures are shattered, *and* grace provides resources to sustain and fund meaning.

God participates in creation, experiencing the pain and joy of life. God cares. For Christians, the miracle of the death and resurrection of Jesus is the affirmation that God, the Holy One, entered creation itself and was not defeated by suffering. We can trust because we know that God is a partner, experiencing our pain and standing with us. Suffering and loss of meaning need not be the last word. Grace is present—hope, vision, and struggle are possible.

Grace and Meaning

Sharon Parks describes the relationship of order, chaos, and grace by using the image of shipwreck.[6] Yearning, catastrophe, and success can overwhelm us. Our meanings become shattered. In such moments we are shipwrecked.

The meanings that sustained us have broken apart. The trustworthy has crashed on the shores of life.

Yet, shipwreck is not always all there is. The crash is very real, but there are also moments of survival. People can draw meanings from their experiences to sustain them. For example, after the death of a loved one, we can feel the pain of loss and yet reenter life. Mildred, whose husband had helped integrate the schools, both experienced loss and honored his vision of social justice.

How can we survive the devastation of shipwreck? Not all people do. Homeless people may lose purpose when the structures they counted on are torn from them. Some people are devastated by the loss of a loved one, never able to reenter life. Others are debilitated by illness. Still others are ground down by oppression. Grace usually does not come as grand rescue from shipwreck. Rather, grace emerges in glimpses of hope and possibility, on which we can draw for meaning. Even in desperate circumstances, a glimpse of hope, a touch of care, or a hint of meaning can call us forward.

Parks writes that faith "is an active dialogue with promise."[7] Faith is both a *meaning-perspective,* through which we organize and confront the world, and also a gracious gift of hope and meaning. Our language contains words that appear to go together: soup and sandwich, hand and glove. The same is true for *amazing* and *grace.* Grace is *amazing.* Grace is God's love and care, freely extended within the world.

First, grace is amazing because it is of God. The Judeo-Christian heritage proclaims its wonder. The Hebrew Bible makes reference to the wonder of grace in terms of "favor." For example, Joseph was cast into jail because of the testimony of Potiphar's wife, yet God bestowed on Joseph steadfast love and favor (Gen. 39:21). The writings of the apostle Paul refer to God's graciousness as mediated through Jesus Christ. Paul closes his letters with a benediction: "The grace of our Lord Jesus Christ be with you" (I Thess. 5:28).

Second, grace is amazing because it is extended to all creation. It is eternal and unceasing. The creation itself is bound together by God's grace. The psalmist echoes repeatedly, "God's steadfast love endures forever." God's amazing gift is abundant, exceeding human expectations. Grace is free, not dependent upon our efforts.

Grace, amazing grace, enables us to trust, to risk, and to seek to make meaning. While we do experience isolation and brokenness, God's grace reconnects us with others. Glimpses of community and care then give us courage to search for meanings. Theologian Rita Nakashima Brock summarizes this power of connectedness:

> To be born open to the presence of others in the world gives us enormous, creative capacity to make life whole. Finding our heart requires a loving presence who helps us search, who is not afraid of the painfulness of the search, and who can mirror back our buried and broken heart, returning us to a healing memory of our earliest pain and need for love.[8]

Making life whole is a task of meaning-making. Faith as gift propels that task.[9] Grace empowers our religious search for meanings that make life whole and connect us to ultimate concerns.

Religion as Source for Meaning

The people on the work trip to Central America were vulnerable. They scanned and reassessed meanings at the core of their lives. A glimpse of meaning came at the parting meal. The last supper became the lens through which their vulnerability was interpreted. Had not that too been a time of vulnerability, when meanings and relationships were questioned? Entering into the sacrament helped them touch their connection with one another and experience God's power. The Christian religious tradition became a resource to fund their search for meaning.

The religious tradition was also central to Jennifer and her Aunt Ellen. At five, Jennifer knew to cry out to God. Yet she questioned when her prayer was not answered. God did not make it possible for her to talk with her grandfather. The church had taught her to communicate with God in prayer; she expected a response. In this case, Jennifer had to discover a different set of expectations for prayer. But the church also gave her stories, concepts, and images, through which she could continue to explore her relationship with God. In other words, both she and the visitors to Central America experienced their religion as funding their meanings and connecting them to God.

In Luke 4, Jesus is described as using the prophecy of Isaiah as a source for his meanings and his understanding of himself. Name some biblical stories that are important to you. What meanings do you draw from these stories? What are some other resources for your meanings (proverbs expressed in families, church beliefs, professional study, etc.)?

On Defining Religion

Religions help us learn how to live in the midst of the deepest and ultimate questions of life. Catherine Albanese, a historian of religion, argues that all religions begin by engaging human boundaries. We experience the boundaries of culture and ask ourselves how we can live within the rituals, laws, and expectations of our cultures. We also experience national boundaries and must learn how to relate to *strangers* with whom we share life on this globe. Moreover, we live within the boundaries of our physical bodies. How do we communicate with others who are outside our feelings, who are different from us, and with whom we seek community? Finally, there are the boundaries of time. How do we learn the wisdom of the past? How do we pass through the life cycle of birth and death? As Albanese summarizes:

> Religious or theological language has always tried to speak about the unspeakable. It has been "limit" language, language that pushed to the edge of human knowledge and tried to talk about what went beyond. Death, judgment, heaven, hell, these were the last things in Christian theology. They were also passes across the boundary of the world we know, attempts to make sense of mysterious realities from a different world.[10]

Albanese distinguishes two types of religions: ordinary and extraordinary religion. *Ordinary religion* is about learning to live within the boundaries of our ordinary world. We learn to accept and cherish the taken-for-granted ways of a culture. Ordinary religion invests the daily processes of meaning-making with ultimate significance.[11] For example, in the United States, "life, liberty, and the pursuit of happiness" are known as God-given "unalienable" rights. For many cultures, the values of hard work and family are divinely instituted. Or in many Asian nations influenced by Confucianism, hierarchies are God given: Respect for elders and the harmony of the social order are expectations of their ordinary religions.

Another explanation of ordinary religion is provided by Robert Bellah, a sociologist of religion, when he calls religion a "gyroscope." Religion grounds the person and the society as they pass through the natural rhythms of living and cultural transition. Religion provides "a stable set of definitions of the world and, correlatively, of the self, so that the transience and crises of life can be faced."[12] Religion, therefore, deals with what is of ultimate significance in life.

However, ordinary religion can become alienating when it confuses cultural patterns with ultimate truths. For instance, emphasis on family values can make single or divorced people feel inadequate. The church's defense of slavery and segregation in the 1800s was alienating. For many "religious" slave owners, inequality and separation were theological truths and therefore unchangeable. Critical distance was lost as slavery became a "God-given" ordering of culture and segregation was defended on religious grounds. Another example is the way that majority groups have sought to control minority groups. Because many U.S. school systems celebrate only the Christian religious holidays, other religions appear to be unimportant.[13] Ordinary religion provides structure for our meaning-perspectives.

The second type of religion, *extraordinary religion,* deals with situations in which the boundaries have been challenged or are not broad enough. Death is crossing a boundary. What will the future be? Cultures, too, have futures. While cultures sustain life, they can limit options and oppress. When we reach out to make a culture more inclusive, we approach an unknown boundary. Challenging the limits of cultural definitions helps people to cross another boundary.

Albanese contends that "the special (theological) language of extraordinary religion maps a landscape that living people have not clearly seen. It gives people names for the unknown and then provides access to the world beyond. . . . It deals with how to negotiate boundaries and still return to the ordinary world."[14] In these situations, we again need a gyroscope to keep us balanced, but it must transcend patterns of taken-for-granted daily life and provide new options.

Another name for this second kind of religion is *prophetic*. The prophetic challenges the alienation and oppression of cultural patterns. It authorizes a search for justice by proclaiming that God is calling the world to new life.[15] Here is the revolutionary character of religion. The Protestant Reformation and the Roman Catholic Counter Reformation are clear examples of religion renewing itself. Both Martin Luther and Ignatius Loyola risked past meanings as they followed the call of prophetic religion. Extraordinary religion opens our meaning-perspectives to a search for the new.

New movements provide new possibilities.[16] The base communities in Latin America are calling churches and societies to be more responsive to the needs of the ordinary people, the poor.[17] The U.S. visitors to Central America were profoundly affected by the sense of community found in these groups and their efforts to humanize life for the people.

Religion deals with both the *ordinary* and the *extraordinary*, with *daily processes* of meaning and with *reconstruction*. Religion addresses both because it confronts ultimate questions—those that are significant for life and the future. Living religiously is living *sub species aeternitatis*, "in light of eternity." Therefore, religion has to do with salvation—with living life holistically and interconnected with the cosmos itself.[18] Religion saves by investing daily meanings with ultimate significance and helping a person know his or her vocation in life. Religion also saves by providing ways of "turning around," of transforming, so that new meanings can be lived.

The religious man Nicodemus is an example of both kinds of religion (John 3:1-10). The religion of his tradition had been enough; it provided order and meaning. Nicodemus knew his place in society. He had an identity and a vocation. But the encounter with Jesus opened him to new questions about the meaning of life. He talked with Jesus at night, hidden from his compatriots.[19] He feared such a conversation would disrupt his place in his society. Older meanings were no longer adequate.

Jesus understood the power of religion to provide order and to transform. He told Nicodemus that he had to be "born again"—that is, made new with new meanings—in this case, of the kingdom of God. Some of Nicodemus' search is recorded in the Gospel. He does not change his mind in the conversation with Jesus, but he later counsels caution to his colleagues who find Jesus threatening. He calls for listening and openness (John 7:50-52). And, even later, he joins with Joseph of Arimathea in preparing Jesus' body for burial (John 19:38-42).

The ways in which religion undergirds daily truth and calls for transformation are clarified in a classic definition of religion by the anthropologist Clifford Geertz. Religion is:

> (1) a system of symbols which acts to (2) establish powerful, pervasive, and long-lasting moods and motivations in [humans] by (3) formulating conceptions of a general order of existence and (4) clothing these conceptions with such an aura of factuality that (5) moods and motivations seem uniquely realistic.[20]

Religion is about the most important things needed for living, what theologian Paul Tillich has called "ultimate concern."[21] Grace and hope are the sources of religion. The experiences in which we touch the boundaries, the limits of our worlds, and discover the search worthwhile are the foundation of religion. Religion is a response to wonder, mystery, and grace. It is grounded in hope-renewing glimpses in the midst of brokenness, depth experiences of love and connectedness, and new possibilities that emerge from boundaries. Religion becomes central to our temples of meaning as we seek to make sense of our feelings and our experiences.

Religions affect the way we order our lives. The popular author Rabbi Harold Kushner suggests this power of religion: "The issue is not what God is like. The issue is what kind of people we become when we attach ourselves to God."[22] The choice profoundly affects the way we live, our ethics. Religions provide key meanings for people. Religions fund meaning-perspectives and give order to the most significant aspects of life.

Religious Knowing and Learning

Albanese contends that religions have four elements: creed, code, cultus, and community.[23] *Creeds* involve stories, belief statements, symbols, and theologies by which people explain their faith.[24] Creeds can be approved statements of faith, like the Westminster Confession of Faith or The Apostle's Creed. Creeds also include paradigmatic stories of the faith, like the passion story of the death and resurrection of Jesus.

Codes are the rules and customs expected of participants in the religion. For Baha'is, the equality of all races is a tenet to be lived. A code for the religions of the Middle Eastern desert was the rule of hospitality—the stranger was to be fed and sheltered.

Cultus includes the ritual and worship practices expected of the devout. For example, Orthodox Jews honor the sabbath by walking to worship. All Jews participate in Yom Kippur, the great day of atonement, when one is reminded of sin, God's forgiveness, and new life.[25]

Finally, religions are embodied in *communities* where people nurture one another and share faith together. The history of Judaism is a profound example of a people who held on to the power of religion by holding on to community, even as they were shoved throughout Europe. Community is a primary educator of faith, as people learn by participating in its creeds, codes, and cultic activities. "Faith normally requires for its proper development a community of believers who support each other in their convictions and aspirations."[26]

Identify, from your own experience, examples of creed, code, cultus, and community.

Religions are learned in many ways. Each of the four elements listed above is an entry point into religious education. People learn as they come to know the beliefs (the creeds, symbols, and stories) of a faith. Luther's catechisms taught many children the Lutheran faith. The Baltimore Catechism was the primary mode of learning the doctrines of the Roman Catholic Church in the U.S. for more than one hundred years.

Others learn a faith by participating in its codes. During the 1960s, many in the U.S. learned the power of African American churches as they participated in marches for justice and heard stories that linked Exodus with the promise of the "American dream" of equality.

For others, the cultic acts of worship and liturgy are powerfully educative. A Muslim, praying five times each day on a prayer rug, communicates the nearness of the Holy One. Finally, communities teach the young and maintain faith as people live together.[27] Amish children learn the ways of their religious group as they dress, work, and live side by side with brothers and sisters in the faith.

Religious knowing is a process akin to creativity. People interpret experiences of grace and brokenness out of the stories, concepts, and images that are crucial for them. *Interpretation is an imaginative process through which we connect images into meanings.* Greeley gives an example of this process in *Religious Imagination.* Religious discourse is like storytelling. We connect experiences we have had with those the religious storyteller is describing.[28] For example, Jesus was a master storyteller. His parables were rooted in the stories and images of his culture. He captured meanings that were alive in the people and enriched their ways of seeing and acting.

Today, for another example, as Christians retell the story of Christ, symbols and liturgy enrich the telling. We respond to both the doctrines and the stories that echo with our lives. As Jesus cried, "So, could you not stay awake with me one hour?" to a sleepy Peter, we remember times of loneliness or betrayal (Matt. 26:40*b*). Our experience resonates with that of Jesus. Through imagination, we are linked to what Greeley calls the "founding experience itself." Therefore, central to people's learning about a religion is that they experience the images, rituals, stories, traditions, practices, and liturgies of a faith, and practice using these sources in theological reflection.

Religious education deals with more than content.[29] It also includes strategies of theological reflection (creed), practices of the religion (code and cultus), and life together in the community of believers (community). Fundamental to learning a religion are experiences of wonder, awe, and joy, and the resources to interpret these experiences. Andrew Greeley poetically summarizes, "Awe, wonder, grace, death, and the apparent presence of otherness in such encounters appeal to, or more appropriately 'seize,' the total personality."[30]

For example, Randy told the story of a service of healing for his mother who was dying of cancer. While the service did not remove her tumor, she proclaimed, even on her death bed, that the service had healed her rage at God and empowered her to face dying. The service renewed her connection with others and with God. The last three months of her life were lived abundantly. Her religion contributed resources that helped her make sense of the mystery she faced. It also provided resources that enabled her son to understand his feelings and her life.

Religion strives to connect us with the Ultimate and enables us to develop an identity and a vocation. Christianity communicates this insight powerfully in the image of the cross. Not only does the cross represent the suffering and death of Jesus (God's full participation in human life, suffering, betrayal, and redemption), it is also a symbol of the incarnation of God as intersecting the earthly.

Through religious education, we affirm the search for meaning in which all humans engage. Religious education is grounded in the efforts of all of us to understand, interpret, and live in light of eternity—to know God intimately and to enhance creation. The challenge to religious education is to be open to the prophetic claim of God who, throughout creation, calls us to meaning, identity, and vocation.

PART TWO

EDUCATING TOWARD VOCATION

CHAPTER FOUR

LIVING IN THE INTERSECTIONS

Learning

Out of our experiences, the building blocks of our lives, we construct our temples of meaning—that is, we attempt to make, discover, and reconstruct meanings into a coherent whole. In the midst of this natural process, we face ultimate questions—ones that have to do with God—especially when we encounter our limits. When current meanings become inadequate for life experience, when the walls of our temples collapse, we may be "shipwrecked" for a time until we can construct or find new, more adequate meanings. Our meanings become the impetus for our vocations, what we must do, how we must live. The learning process is the topic of this chapter.

One of the times which often requires meaning-making is the birth of a child. A group of young mothers regularly gathers around a church classroom table. One day as they shared their faith journeys, several related the powerful experience of God's presence when first holding their new babies.

Sue explained, "I was alone in a room after the delivery and it was quiet. I felt the warmth of God's presence wrapped around me like a soft blanket. I breathed a prayer of thanksgiving for my new baby."

Later in the conversation, Meg raised a question: "Is God only in the good things?"

Jane said, "I wonder just what God's power is. I don't expect God to provide a parking place when I go downtown."

"Neither do I," added Kathy. "But I do pray to God to help me not get so angry with my in-laws." The conversation was moving toward "critical" thinking about their ideas of who God is and how God is present in the world. They began to think theologically.

Meg commented, "For me, it's like the hymn, 'I Need Thee Every Hour.' I have little conversations with God all day long. They help me get through the day." These women were beginning to reflect on their meanings. Their experience and the church's traditions inform them. They are learning about faith and vocation.

From Meaning to Vocation

Although acquiring information (adding to our meaning-schemes) is one aspect of learning, more fundamentally, learning involves change in the structure of our temples of meaning (meaning-perspectives). Mezirow, for example, defines learning as a process of "construing or appropriating a new or revised interpretation of the meaning of an experience as a guide to awareness, feeling, and action."[1] Learning is using meanings to understand experiences and to shape our responses. Learning moves from meaning to vocation.

Joan, a minister of youth and music in a large church, spoke of how she learned more clearly who she is and what she believes the church must be. A new pastor unilaterally had changed the church's style of worship. In the staff meetings, as she resisted some of the changes, Joan learned what, for her, were essential ingredients of worship.

"In the presence of the 'no,' the 'yes' becomes defined," she said. She remembered important and meaningful liturgies which she could not give up. The current worship experiences connected to remembered worship. The result was learning with more clarity how the liturgy should be constructed. She wondered whether she could stay in this church, where her word seemed to mean so little. Learning occurred. Her interpretation of experience resulted in a search for a new understanding of who she is and what she must do.

Learning Is Rooted in Life Experience

Experience is the impetus and content of learning. Education is a context for facilitating learning. Learning begins with new experiences connecting to remembered meanings (that is, connecting new experience to past meaning-schemes). For instance, in arithmetic, we learn what numbers "mean" and build on those meanings to learn the process of addition. When we move from addition to multiplication, we learn that multiplying is a way of adding. We have attributed an old meaning to a new experience. (Our meaning-scheme is adequate for the new situation.)

A similar but more complex process of learning takes place when a family gathers for a funeral. As they tell stories of the deceased, each family member begins with his or her own interpretation of the person's life. Each person then either validates the interpretation or reconstructs it in the conversation. Stories often tap through our meaning-schemes to also address and reveal our meaning-perspectives.

Yet, when new experiences do not fit remembered

meanings, we may try to ignore the experience and resist learning. Several in the young-mothers' group habitually thanked God for the good things of life, but they had not considered whether this meant that God was also responsible for the painful. They discounted experiences that did not fit comfortably with their expectation of a loving God. To attend to the question of God's responsibility would have required the reassessment of their meanings.

Occasionally, an experience radically disrupts our expectations. We may be "shipwrecked" for a time as our meanings are being transformed. In shipwreck, past meanings are inadequate. We are set adrift, required to learn new meanings in order to survive the chaos and danger of the open sea. Broken relationships, such as divorce, often precipitate shipwreck and transformation.

Peggy, a divorced woman with two young sons, asked repeatedly: "Why did this happen? How can I support myself and my sons? Who am I if I am not a wife?" She felt cast adrift, with no confidence of survival. For Peggy, learning did bring a new structure which included a career and a reclaimed sense of self-worth; yet the transformation was not easy. It was filled with pain and anguish.

The Processes of Learning

Learning theorists focus on the way learning interacts with past and present experience. Mezirow, for example, says that learning begins with perception. In the complex and chaotic world of everyday life, only small bits of which we perceive, we choose to what we will attend. Our blinders, our past meanings, and our meaning-perspectives often affect what we will see. For example, as I listen to and watch a friend making a speech, I am aware of a tightness in his throat and a raised vocal pitch. A speaker unknown to me exhibits many similar clues, but I ignore them, because I have no context to which they relate. My knowledge focuses my perception.

Perception then calls us to scan: I ask what my friend's vocal clues mean. I scan by "exploring, differentiating, recognizing, feeling, intuiting, and imagining" from among the information, feelings, symbols, and possibilities in my repertoire of meaning.[2] I sort through the meaning-schemes at my disposal to understand what is happening.

Finally, I construe meaning by linking what is perceived with the concepts and categories I have scanned (with my meaning-schemes). As I listen to my friend, I name the raised pitch, tight gestures, and shortness of breath "anxiety"; and I learn more about my friend. Learning links experience with concepts. For instance, the woman who had just given birth could not have named the warmth she felt as the presence of God, were she not acquainted with the concept of God as loving and comforting presence. Naming completes the process of learning.

However, when past categories and concepts are inadequate, learning calls us back to scanning in order to seek out new concepts and categories. We explore, for example, by reading books; talking to other people about their concepts and experiences; and by probing our images, and even our dreams, to seek ways to understand experience and make meaning. The young women in the mothers' group began to explore new images and concepts for understanding the presence of evil in God's world. They had to search beyond their past understandings.

Another learning theorist, theologian James Loder, identifies five steps in a learning event which transform (reshape) a meaning-perspective: (1) a conflict, or dissonance between current meanings and experience; (2) an interlude for scanning, searching for possible solutions to the dissonance; (3) a constructive act of imagination, an intuitive insight; (4) the "ah ha!"—the feeling of release and resolution; and (5) interpretation by which we test our insights with others and move toward the future.[3] For Loder, images empower the learning process. The images provide the building blocks to remake our temples. Interpretation can occur through story or concept. And scanning surveys our past stories, concepts, and images.

Scanning and intuitive insight appear prominently in many stories of people being called to ministry, especially in those for whom it is a second career. Adrienne (chapter 1) found that teaching school did not satisfy her desire to carry on dialogue about ultimate questions (the dissonance). Her scanning had been going on for a long time while she felt dissatisfied with her career. She searched her skills, her knowledge, and her identity. Then the intuitive insight occurred at a workshop on Christian education.

"All the pieces of my life came together and made sense in the calling to ministry," she said. Suddenly, to Adrienne's relief (the ah ha!), the call was clear. Further exploration and interpretation occurred as she decided to remain in teaching, but to move to a college where she could better express her faith.

Meaning-making is a learning process. We remember, reconstruct, and are transformed. Oftentimes, new experiences are congruent and easily connected with already existing meanings. Our meaning-perspectives are not bothered, and our meaning-schemes are adequate. For many of us, worship is often like that. The familiar and beloved phrases of the hymn or liturgy help us to interpret life experience.

At other times, in order to learn or interpret our

experiences, we must reshape former meanings. According to an older man who had been attending Sunday school for most of his adult life:

> When you're the teacher [of the class] I guess you get more out of it, but you don't get a chance to give as much thought as you like to any one statement. I'd rather have someone else be the teacher. I have more time to think about it, mull it over. That's where discussion in a class comes. You have to find out what the others believe. Sometimes they're just lookin' from a different point. It may be that I'm kind of off on a tangent too. It's one of the most important things in my life. You put the time into it to get something out of it.

Sometimes remembered meanings provide an interpretation that is sufficient. Yet, "sometimes they're just lookin' from a different point." The different point of view calls us to reconstruct our meanings. We add to our meaning-schemes. And sometimes we learn that we may be "kind of off on a tangent." Our meanings may need to be transformed. Our meaning-perspectives must be reshaped.

While no one model of learning is entirely adequate for the complexity of human experience, we know that learning occurs only when the process helps us to understand or legitimate life experiences. *If education is to be effective in facilitating learning, it must take into account both the structures of perception (meaning-perspectives) and the content of our interpretations (meaning-schemes).*

Learning occurs in life. Models of learning which have school as the only image must be abandoned. We face new experiences—whether it be long division or the death of a beloved aunt—and interpret them in relation to current meanings. Experience becomes knowledge for the learner only when the learner interprets and acts upon it. Neither the experience of the educator nor information in books will provide learning, unless a connection is made to a person's meanings.

Religious Learning

Religious learning, too, is inseparable from life experience. Religious learning is about meaning—the fullest and deepest meanings, which connect us with the cosmos and God. In other words, religious learning is interpreting life in relation to ultimate questions, and living a life wholly connected to others and to God. We use our meanings to interpret experience. Because of the depth of religious questions, religious learning is often about reconstructing meanings or reshaping temples of meaning.

Religious educators, in turn, cannot respond to efforts at meaning-making with integrity, mutuality, or relevance, unless we take seriously the meanings and questions that are alive for people. Richard Olson, a Lutheran educator, worries that the educational practices of churches are not sufficiently rooted in life experience, nor is God adequately trusted: "In local congregations, the denial of the realities of the lives of men and women within the congregation, community, and the world bespeaks little faith in God's future, as well as little trust in the possibilities of working and dealing with the realities."[4]

Human efforts at meaning-making occur in the midst of the chaotic, perplexing realities of human experience. Therefore, experience is the foundation for religious learning.

Religious Learning Connects Us to Traditions

The people in the group that celebrated the impromptu Eucharist in Central America (chapter 3) were awash in feelings and images they could scarcely put into words, but which called them into new understandings of the presence of God in the world. They were able to name the shared cup of coffee as Eucharist because of remembered experiences of Eucharist in their religious tradition. They discovered afresh (learned) the meaning of the Eucharist, of community, and of God's grace. Because of this new experience, they enlarged and reshaped their religious heritages.

Travis, the conscientious objector (chapter 1), found that seminary helped him voice some of the questions that lurked at the edge of his consciousness. The learning that occurred for him that year involved interpreting his experiences in the Fellowship of Christian Athletes in light of his new seminary experiences. Travis was confused as he felt the dissonance between these religious traditions. The atmosphere, the curriculum, the worship, and the relationships of seminary encouraged Travis to work on meaning questions. A small reflection group in which he participated also responded to the struggle and supported him that year. Eventually, Travis found the dissonance so uncomfortable that he left seminary. He could not integrate the old meanings with the new experiences. The wholeness he sought came only later, when he completed his written defense as a conscientious objector.

Religious traditions consist of witness from the past. Witnesses proclaim to us the interpretations they made as they sought to respond to ultimate questions. While traditions are sometimes in tension with the struggle for meaning in the present, the process of interpreting experience is dynamic. Traditions touch past experience and offer options for the present. Past and present reach into the future. Traditions provide resources (images, stories, and theological processes of decision-making) to interpret experiences and discern God's call.

Religious learning comes to dynamic fruition as vocation. We act out our meanings in regard to views of ultimate good and values. Religious traditions focus our reflection as we seek to know who we are (identity) and what we are called to do (vocation). Human beings are always in process. The trajectory is toward greater wholeness in life and a more faithful vocation. Each of us seeks integration of our understandings, feelings, and actions. We long to find ways to be fully what we can be. We struggle to create temples of meaning whose walls are sturdy and will stand the test of time. Each temple is formed by traditions, cultures, and histories. Therefore, we learn that living in relationship and community with others means respecting their temples of meaning, forged from different traditions, cultures, and histories. Religious learning draws from the witnesses of the past as we seek to be faithful to God in the present.

Religious Learning Occurs in the "Intersection"

Mary Elizabeth Moore, theologian and educator, argues that meaning-making happens at an "intersection," the place where life experiences touch. In the intersection are "not only the Bible and the present life experience of individuals, but parents, church folk, the historical church tradition, the fears and hopes for the future of the world, the culture in which the church exists, the issues of the global village, and God. That intersection is a big place. It is an awesome place."[5]

The intersection for religious learning is filled with our temples of meaning, and with questions, experiences, concepts, stories, and images we have newly encountered. The intersection is not the simple crossing of two roads. It is like a congested urban intersection, with several streets converging and traffic moving in many directions. Some streets are one-way—entrance is prohibited. Others are broad with well-marked lanes, while still others are narrow and winding, so that their destinations are unclear.

Identify a point of change in your life. Draw an intersection and indicate the forces that influenced the direction you chose to take.

Because so much is present in the intersection, Moore argues, religious learning always involves both continuity (remembering) and change (reconstructing and transforming). We bring our past experiences and meanings (our traditions) to the intersection, but we always bring the present and future as well. We are dynamic. The complexity of our life intersections makes change and refocusing possible and inevitable.

Our fullness as humans is in the intersection—our experiences, traditions, hopes, and limitations. Theologian Cornel West writes about the brokenness and possibility in each individual: "This dialectic of imperfect products and transformative practice, of prevailing realities and negation, of human depravity and human dignity, of what is and the not-yet constitutes the Christian dialectic of human nature and human history."[6]

Both our dignity and our depravity are present in the intersection. Depravity, our sinful nature, comes to the intersection in the form of our unwillingness to acknowledge our incompleteness and dependence. Dignity comes from the not yet realized possibilities of transformation. In the intersection, we must reclaim our past, with its sinfulness, as we reach toward transforming the future.

Also at the intersection are others and their traditions and experiences. For theologian Henry Young, the intersection is the whole created world, as well as all human cultures. The elements in this ecosystem function in a complex organization. We are interdependent. All parts must be taken into account because all parts are inextricably connected. Seeking wholeness means moving to end exclusion, oppression, and hierarchy.[7] All of us need to be together to live in this ecosystem.

God is present in the intersection. The creative power we know as God's grace undergirds the ecosystem. It invites us to risk living into the future and calls us to justice and integrity. The lively presence of God energizes meaning.

When we come to the intersection, transformation is always possible; reconstruction often occurs. We encounter so many different meanings. One instance of change caused by the intersection is the struggle over the celebration of Columbus Day. Schoolchildren used to recite that Columbus *discovered* America in 1492, but we are beginning to reconstruct the meanings of origin and discovery as we attend to the life experiences and dignity of indigenous peoples. The future is changed as colonialism is called into question. Successive meanings, when known more fully, move us toward greater wholeness as persons.

Wholeness Is the Goal of Religious Learning

Wholeness includes our relationship to the Holy, to others with whom we share the earth, and to our inner selves. The first dimension of wholeness is to seek to live *"wholly" connected with God*—increasingly open to the God who sustains and nurtures life and lures us forward toward recreating the world. We can be open to the search for wholeness because God journeys with us. The search is intense and faithful as we seek to discern God's call to vocation. Our temples of meaning are potentially opened up, examined, and expanded, because God's call changes commitments.

Theologian Jurgen Moltmann uses the metaphor of passion for life to express this holistic living. Passion for life comes from the Bible's description of God. God's passion reached out to all creation, seeking liberation, justice, and new life. Moreover, the passion of Jesus, his suffering—experienced in life, death, and resurrection—renewed the world. Jesus' passion calls us to live in light of God's transforming possibilities. For Moltmann,

> That which abides in the passion of life, in the midst of living and dying, is love, the mysterious center of life and death, the passionate yes to life and the passionate no to the negation of life. Apathy is a terrible temptation. Promising to spare us death, it in fact takes away our life. It spreads the rigor of corpses and concrete around itself. Love makes life a passion.[8]

God's passion often calls us to be transformed, to live passionately, more deeply connected with others.

We breathe, eat, find shelter, and know ourselves *together and interconnected,* the second dimension of wholeness. While we experience separation from others and, in our sin, separate ourselves from others, separation is ultimately an illusion. Attempts to know ourselves, disconnected from our physical bodies and the world ecosystem, are futile. The dichotomy of spiritual and material does not exist. We know ourselves only in relation to others who give us fellowship and to the world that sustains us.[9] Thus, wholeness calls us to live in just relationships with creation. Being passionate about life means loving life, working to say yes to life. A biblical word for this experience is *shalom:* Since God desires health, justice, love, and peace for all of creation, we too are called to work for health, justice, love, and peace.

The third dimension of wholeness is *personal:* To live whole means increasingly to accept more and more parts of ourselves. We accept and explore our stories, feelings, limitations, needs, commitments, fears, gifts, and hopes. We probe deeply into the unique creatures that we are. The clichéd mid-life crisis is often an attempt to reclaim the more expressive or spiritual aspects of ourselves that have been too long ignored. The new haircut and casual clothes may be concrete expressions of lost parts of ourselves, as is rediscovering the ability to cry or pray, asking others for support, or learning to speak our convictions in public.

To be whole, we need, as Parker Palmer says, both contemplation and action. Contemplation (critical reflection) unveils "illusions that masquerade as reality." We confront the illusions (and sins) by which we have lived. Meaning-perspectives are opened to scrutiny. Cracks form in our temples of meaning. Some of the cracks that are often unveiled are our insistence that we can control others' meanings and our belief that we can escape our embeddedness in the world. True living is related living.

Therefore, to act is to co-create: "We not only express what is in us and help give shape to the world; we also receive what is outside us, and reshape our inner selves. When we act, the world acts back, and we and the world are co-created."[10] We are inextricably connected to the earth and sustained by its power. We face the future together.

Religious learning occurs at the intersection of the realities of our lives and the ultimate. Religious learning shapes our identities and vocations toward wholeness. When we live with passion, we risk opening our meanings to reconstruction and transformation.[11] However, we risk that change knowing that God participates with us. God loves life and is building connections of justice and hope. The joy of living is that we find community on the journey; we find ourselves, others, the rest of creation, and God.

Learning at the Intersection

The intersection is rich. Indeed, as Moore says, it is an awesome place, filled with people, traditions, artifacts, and stories. The young mothers' group (chapter 4) finds their lives enlarged by the others they meet around the table. Their world is enriched as the traditions of the faith are explored, experiences with their families shared, and cherished traditions from their pasts revealed. They may be transformed as they seek to understand that God is active in their lives.

Communities too may be transformed by the intersection. Chen, for example, learned to bridge two worlds. Through him, his friends and family learned of each culture's deeply held convictions about life. While not always understanding each other, they were influenced by the contact. The school Chen attended has been significantly influenced by immigration. Many languages are now spoken. The school is open to differences that its leaders and students could not have imagined ten years earlier. The school also has conflicts which threaten to divide it. But at the same time, conflict can offer possibilities for new life.

The past brings a continuity of meanings. However, the present often requires that the past meanings be reinterpreted. The future can offer new possibilities. Given that the goal of religious learning is greater wholeness, what elements facilitate transformative learning?

> Learning to be whole requires:
>   Hospitable and Just Space
>   Interpreters Working Among Interpreters
>   (Mutuality)
>   Practicing God's Presence

Hospitable and Just Space

The first element of an intersection for religious learning is hospitable and just space. In hospitable space, we are welcomed into the conversation about meanings. We are accepted and safe. Parker Palmer describes hospitality: "Hospitality means receiving each other, our struggles, our newborn ideas, with openness and care. It means creating an ethos in which the community of troth [the pledging of commitment] can form, the pain of truth's transformations be borne."[12] Hospitality is inviting; guests are welcomed as if they were members of the family. Their ideas, needs, and values are heard. Palmer clarifies:

> To be inhospitable to strangers or strange ideas, however unsettling they may be, is to be hostile to the possibility of truth. . . . [Therefore] a learning space needs to be hospitable not to make learning painless but to make the painful things possible, things without which no learning can occur—things like exposing ignorance, testing tentative hypotheses, challenging false or partial information, and mutual criticism of thought.[13]

With hospitality, we receive one another as guests and are open to the gifts each brings.

As long as we fearfully protect our possessions, prejudices, knowledge, or power, we cannot reach out to others in openness and justice. We cannot be transformed toward wholeness. As Henri Nouwen says, "Someone who is filled with ideas, concepts, opinions and convictions cannot be a good host. There is no inner space to listen, no openness to discover the gift of the other."[14] The stranger is treated as neighbor, bringing new meanings which open our own cherished meanings to scrutiny.

Therefore, hospitable space is just, because it honors the whole presence of each one standing in an intersection. The ecosystem concept of Henry Young illuminates the meaning of "just space." Justice occurs only when the intersection takes into account the needs of the whole of creation. The meanings of any individual or culture affect, and are affected by, the existence of the whole ecosystem.

Hospitable space is receptive, welcoming, and affirming, but also confrontational. Critical awareness, seeing both the power of systems to control and the options for freedom, is possible only when we open ourselves to hear those who are different. We must listen carefully to the voices of those who are powerless or have been marginalized by our culture. Differences are claimed, not minimized. Hospitality affirms that each of us will sing our own songs, speak our own languages, and dance our own dances, but in relationship. Since we know our differences, we are able to critique our songs, languages, and dances, and revise them in light of the gifts and support of the other, the stranger.

Using neighborhood publications, newspapers, and public-service announcements, identify your community's issues and concerns. What do *hospitality and justice* entail for your congregation? How do you *interpret* these issues and concerns? How can you *practice God's presence?*

Interpreters Among Interpreters

The second element of the intersection for religious learning is the understanding that all people are interpreters. In the intersection, we become one another's teachers, guides, and mentors. Our meanings are personal. We can only "know" the slice of experience that our meaning-perspectives bring to awareness. In addition, each of us interprets that slice.[15] The personal temples of meaning in which we dwell are shaped by constructs and traditions appropriated from our cultures and histories. Therefore, no two of us will experience life in the same way; no two of us will rely on the same meanings. Each of us is an interpreter among interpreters.

Too often we have seen teachers as the only knowledgeable ones; teachers too are interpreters. We all enter the space with others as seekers of truth. The teacher who comes to share *the only truth* has assumed a power not warranted. The teacher has unique stories and experiences which influence the way she or he makes meaning. Yet, all others in the intersection also have unique stories and experiences.

Each interpreter, including the teacher, stands in the intersection, alive to the possibility of transformation. Thus, listening is a key task—to be open to another's "strange" view may lead to a new truth. In addition, the teacher/interpreter, standing alongside other interpreters, facilitates exploring the dimensions of our intersections as he or she models an openness to change.

Practicing the Presence of God

A third element of the intersection is the practicing of God's presence. Brother Lawrence, a simple man who spent most of his life working in a monastery kitchen and shoe-repair shop, became known as a holy person. When people asked about his method of holiness, his response was surprising: "I have given up all my non-obligatory devotions and prayers and concentrate on being always in His holy presence." Lawrence's method consisted of "simple attentiveness and loving gaze upon God . . . or to put it more clearly, an habitual, silent and secret conversation of the soul with God."[16] For Brother Lawrence, the task of a person seeking faithfulness is to practice the presence of God, or to consider experience in light of God. He challenged, albeit kindly, the rigid systems demanded of monks by suggesting, instead, that during work, daily activities, and even devotions, people should "savor" God.

Ethicist Margaret Farley provides an expansion of the concept of presence. A synonym for presence is *abide*. We promise to abide in a relationship with another. In other words, we will "be there," even into the future. To be present is to pay attention and seek to nurture a relationship. Farley provides a contrast between *presence* and *constancy*. *Constancy* "legally" fulfills a promise; *presence*, however, is working to overcome "staleness" and keep a relationship alive. Therefore, the activity of practicing presence, in human relationships and with God, seems to have three characteristics: (1) nurturing and renewing a commitment; (2) entering deeply into its pain; and (3) mutuality, knowing that we are not alone.[17]

To understand the concept of *practicing presence*, all we need do is look at a loving relationship. People who care about each other take time to be with each other, to tell stories and make meanings in light of each other. For instance, though a couple in a commuter marriage need to communicate while apart, when together, they need to reconnect by sharing their experiences. They remake the meaning of the time apart in light of their relationship.

Religious learning involves discerning the presence of God, calling us into meaning and ministry.[18] Practicing presence involves remembering and hoping into the future, risking to enter deeply into pain and relationship with trust, and communicating and working together. When we practice the presence of God, we seek to be receptive: We both look for God's presence and expect to be surprised.

Identify the ways you seek to practice God's presence in your life. Among those you know well, who seems to practice God's presence? Describe.

Implications

Religious education is a context which facilitates religious learning. It is a hospitable and just space in which authentic human beings, including those who have been called "teachers" and "learners," may consider together their life experiences and meanings; in which remembered meanings may be laid alongside new experiences for interpretation or transformation; and in which we expect God's presence to abide. The goal is vocation, living in wholeness, in meaningful and just relationships. We seek to live out our meanings in the social order.

We educate *on behalf of the church* when we proclaim the faith of the church, community, and tradition. Sharing meanings from the tradition enables persons to affirm their "membership" in the Christian fellowship. On behalf of the church, we are educating Christians when we pass on the creed, code, and cultus to each new generation, thereby ensuring the continuity of the Christian religion. We also seek to build up the community of the church.

We educate *as the church* when we legitimate an individual's experiences. We empower persons to see their experiences in light of the presence of God and convert their meanings into actions. We educate as the church when we help people participate in the remaking of the faith tradition. Education can provide alternative frames of reference, or fresh images and stories that can help a person move toward greater wholeness.

New experiences may call us into transforming both our personal meanings and those of the tradition. But mutuality and increasing openness toward ourselves, creation, and God are keys to risking these new possibilities. Grace and revelation may reach in and touch us unbidden. In Mark, Jesus cried both for his disciples and for the religious leaders of the day because they could not recognize God's acts which surrounded them. We expect God's eruptive, enfolding, creative, transformative presence among us. Religious education is a setting for addressing the mystery, grace, and joy which will break into our lives.

As Palmer says, we create "a space in which obedience to truth may be practiced."[19] To those who sit in our churches, we offer food in the form of the rich Christian tradition—its stories, images, and doctrines. Practicing truth requires that we encounter the alternative mean- ing-perspectives of those who will not yet enter the doors of the church. The encounter may be painful as we discover that we limit truth and our need for transforma- tion. Religious teaching helps us discern God's call and our response.

CHAPTER FIVE

HAVENS OF HOSPITALITY

Learning in the Church

The neighborhood was deteriorating. A third of the stores in the business zone were closed, and those that were not had barred windows. Several of the brownstone flats in the surrounding blocks displayed boarded windows. Neighbors usually remained behind their locked doors. The area was known for drug sales and gang activity.

Bethel Church was located a block-and-a-half south of the business strip. The church showed wear. Paint was peeling from the overhang, and a sooty stain covered the bricks. Broken glass littered the streets around it. A scratched metal door provided a side entrance to the church. Scrawled on it was "Neighborhood Club," and below, "Ring bell to enter."

Through the door, a stairway descended to a basement, where sounds of joy reverberated. On the wall of the stairway was a bright mural featuring pictures of Martin Luther King, Jr., Malcolm X, and members of the congregation at work. The door provided an entrance to the after-school program for children and teens.

The church was a haven of hospitality and hope, with a soup kitchen, a clothing center, and a job-counseling program. It had led efforts to challenge businesses that degraded the area by selling drug paraphernalia. It had brought national leaders to meet those who lived in these desperate social conditions.

After each school day, the church sponsors the Neighborhood Club: a tutoring program, a rape-counseling center, and a "spiritual maturity" group for teens. The club is directed by a young man once a member of the leading neighborhood gang, who says, "I've got capital with the kids. They know I've been there." On the walls of the basement are lists of awards the church gives to the young people as they earn grades and participate in community outreach missions. Staffing the center is a team of four, including a cook—all from the congregation.

Jamal says, "We are not going to give them [the teenagers] to the gangs. You have to stand up."

Sandy echoes, "I'm supposed to be here."

In a separate room, the "spiritual maturity" group for teenage boys is held.[1] The east wall is filled with a mural, more like an outline, which the teens painted, listing the ways society tries to entice young people away from their faith. As the boys talk about the mural, they discuss their schools, their hopes, their responsibilities to the neighborhood, their struggle to resist gangs, and their faith. They are articulate. They talk about their failures and the chance that God is giving them. They also talk about racism.

"It's sin," Trey declares. "Power and money can destroy us. They want to keep us in our place." Their words are angry as they defy racism, but their words also reflect the hope and inclusivity of the gospel.

"We are going to have to work," asserts Derrick. "God wants us to make a difference." These teenagers probe beneath the surface of social problems. They are learning what it means to be created in the image of God. While they do not know all the formal words of theology, they are participating in theological reflection and social criticism as they witness to the power of faith to call us to wholeness.

The program at Bethel works at the intersection of faith and life. Young people gather in a hospitable and just space, learning to live with meaning and hope. They laugh, study, reflect on their experience, critique the social world, talk about how faith makes a difference, and pray. Bethel has expanded its education beyond the typical Sunday school and youth fellowship. Education permeates the congregation in its study, its worship, and its community action, while its very walls proclaim that life and faith intersect. For the people of Bethel, religion is a set of stories, concepts, and images that keeps them balanced as they engage life. It is their gyroscope (chapter 3). The education of their church connects the people to God's incarnation, grace, and love.

We all seek meanings to guide our lives. In North America, we seem thrown on our own resources to make meaning. As Robert Bellah and his co-authors have pointed out in *Habits of the Heart,* "The self-reliant American is required not only to leave home but to 'leave church' as well."[2] We pay a price for such autonomy. When our temples of meaning fall, we find ourselves isolated.

Those of us concerned about education and religion realize the pain of facing life's shipwrecks with no resources but our own. The church, its worship, its fellowship, and its Sunday school can be key places to seek identity and vocation. Search Institute investigated Christian education effectiveness in six major denominations. It was affirmed that "Christian education is the most important aspect of congregational life for helping people of all ages grow in their faith."[3] Nevertheless, while the church may be a powerful resource, too often it misses its opportunity.

A study of St. Stephens Church in Washington, D.C., disclosed that the members did not experience the church as a hospitable space for intersecting faith and life. They declared that their church was one of the last places they would share their religious experiences, because people would think them strange.[4] The church must engage with passion the questions of meaning and vocation at the intersections of people's lives. We must be open to people's experiences, open to the world, and open to the gospel.

Settings for Learning

Within Bethel, the children and teens found a safe, hospitable, and just space in which to intersect the experiences of their lives with the lively presence of God. The church honored their life experiences, challenged the powerful socializing pressures of community and nation, and helped them struggle to understand God's call. The church building itself became a sanctuary for equipping the youth to engage their world. They are honored as interpreters whose stories are being united to the story of the faith.

The church can be a primary setting for discovering and making religious meaning. The whole life of the congregation can be a setting for learning. Three such settings are worship, Sunday school, and intensive small groups.

Hospitality, Interpretation, and Presence in Worship

The people around Alice were startled. The four-year-old raised her dinner roll, looked up to heaven, broke the roll, and dipped it into her juice. On that day, as she began her meal, she broke her bread in God's presence. Her actions proclaimed that the events of Sunday morning had profoundly affected her.

The church was a merger of three congregations—United Methodist, United Church of Christ, and United Presbyterian. While the union had occurred ten years earlier, the three congregations were still working to become one. They had two worship services: An experimental 9:00 service, which some called frivolous; and a traditional, some said stuffy, 11:00 service. The church's worship life evidenced that tensions remained within the new congregation.

Three times a year, both services were merged into a celebration: Easter Sunday; an Advent service; and the annual (anniversary) meeting. This was the Sunday of the anniversary meeting. At 10:00 A.M., the whole congregation gathered for worship to celebrate their life together. A congregational dinner and meeting were followed by an opportunity for the members to evaluate how the church's mission had been fulfilled during the past year.

The worship service was a pageant. The theme of mission called the people to worship. They confessed their failures before one another and before God. They heard the scriptures read and preached, as they considered what it meant to be God's people in mission. Then each group in the church brought forth an offering of their work: a wooden staff from a school they supported in Africa; pictures from a work camp; music by the choir; a gift of money, collected by the children for a local settlement house. Other gifts followed as they celebrated their church.

Then bread, baked by the preschool class, and the wine of the Eucharist were brought forth. The elements were blessed, and all ate together around the table, as children and adults served each other. The Eucharist was their connection to one another and to the tradition, in anticipation of the meal they would share together in God's kingdom.

The service emphasized unity. Serious issues faced them that afternoon as they planned for the new year, but Alice gave them hope. She had incarnated the focus of the day. Today was God's day. They knew that it was hard to be loyal to a congregation while they still held onto denominational differences. Yet, their efforts at ecumenism could be a proclamation of the unity of God's people.

This annual celebration was not planned as an educational event, but it was powerfully educative. When we think of education as providing a hospitable and just space, where interpreters practice the presence of God at the intersections of their lives, we are empowered to see and engage the natural patterns of education within a congregation. The worship service of this merged church celebrated and shared its strengths and weaknesses. Moreover, each group symbolically communicated their contribution to the whole at the same time their diversity was honored.

The annual meeting encouraged people to accept limitations and claim new directions. The people were honored as interpreters of the faith. The practice of presence occurred as the people evaluated and celebrated their life as a congregation, in light of God's call. The format allowed for a remembering of the past and a projecting into the future, as they sought to discern where and how they were faithfully responding to God.

Worship is a powerful moment in the life of a people when the tradition, the lively presence of God, the experiences of daily life, and visions for the future intersect. It is an example of how all education is relating one's identity and vocation to the presence and call of a God who is intimately involved with people. Alice's breaking of the bread was a symbol of the congregation's embodying of the real presence of grace and love.

> Think about a worship service that was important for you. Identify what you learned. What role did that service play in forming your identity and vocation?

Hospitality, Interpretation, and Presence in Sunday School

A young-adult Sunday school class was founded in 1985 with ten members. It now has more than fifty. The growth of the class can be traced to the friendship of the participants, as well as to the church's growth. Yet, it also was affected by two crisis events.

In 1987, one of the members of the class was killed in a plane crash. The class rallied around the wife, sitting with her in the intensive-care waiting room. Members shared together what was, for many, a first experience with death.

A year later they faced another crisis of meaning when a young mother suffered a heart attack and subsequently underwent by-pass surgery. "As her life hung in the balance, the class again rallied around, bringing food for the family, visiting at the hospital, and offering prayers on her behalf."[5]

While every class is unique, this one is like many others where caring communities have formed. On the surface, the people seem similar—young to middle-age adults, attractive, well-educated. Yet, their meanings remain diverse. Some look for authorities to tell them what to believe. One person, for example, said:

> The more I read the Bible and about the Bible, the more curious I am as to how God really feels. What does He

really think, and what kind of action is right, and what kind
of action am I supposed to take? When I took other
people's word for it, the surface information I had, it was a
lot easier to know the answers.[6]

Others are excited by diverse ideas. "I do love to hear
other people's views and I do grow from them. . . . There
are so many views in our Sunday school, so many open
views. I don't want to change to their views because I don't
believe them. But it's OK for you to have them."[7]

In this class, four reasons for attending were expressed.
First, traditional role expectations: Because they always
had, or because they wanted their children to experience
the church. One person said, "When [Sunday school]
becomes part of your life, you just keep doing it."[8] Just as
we keep in touch with a child away at college or with
friends many miles away, to keep our lives connected, the
church provides a setting to connect our lives to God.

Second, social reasons: "You find friends"; "We like the
people"; "I see my Sunday school family every week. I
don't go for the growth. I go for the social. I want to go
because I care about you and I know you care about me.
And I know you'll support me."[9] These comments reveal
that we are not alone. We make meaning and discover
vocation with help from our friends in faith.

Third, to hear religious meanings expressed: One
person said that the people in the class helped "solidify my
thinking." Another, "It's good to hear the way others
think."[10] The Sunday school provides a place to hear the
faith tradition. From others, we learn new ideas, new
doctrines, and new problems which become resources for
our meaning making. We need to hear the stories,
concepts, and images of the faith. We need the witness of
others who have found the faith significant.

Fourth, to express faith: The Sunday school can be a

place to share pain and joy, and to test interpretations in a supportive community. One woman said, "Since I have been coming to Sunday school I have owned my beliefs, I guess because I have been able to talk about beliefs and convictions in the class."[11] The Sunday school gives us a place to practice exploring, discerning, and making sense.

How does the experience of this class express hospitality, interpretation, and practicing presence? The Sunday school can become a community where people share and explore the issues of their lives and vocations. This class is a setting for the "search for a faith to live by." To be this, the Sunday school must take "the realities of people's lives seriously." People seek confirmation of meanings. We need to explore at the intersection of the faith tradition, life experience, and God's grace; practice together methods of theological reflection; and seek to call one another into ministry.

The Search Institute study of Christian education discovered five characteristics of educational effectiveness:

1. Creates a sense of community in which people help one another develop faith and values.
2. Uses life experiences as occasions for spiritual insight.
3. Applies faith to political and social issues.
4. Respects the importance and uniqueness of each person's faith journey.
5. Encourages independent thinking and questioning.[12]

These factors were honored in this class. That is not the case in all classes, nor is it the case every week in a particular class. All classes have taboo issues and sometimes ignore people's pain. Moreover, the Sunday school sometimes does not encourage the intensity needed for exploration. Congregations need to vary educational settings—Sunday school, intensive small groups, action-reflection groups, and worship—all these may be opportunities for learning. The way we are open to one another, explore the faith, dwell in our meanings together, and find support in the journey of life is decisive.

Describe a Sunday school class that has been important for you. What reasons did you have for participating? How did the class help you understand your identity and/or vocation?

Hospitality, Interpretation, and Presence in Small Groups

Small intensive-learning groups have always been part of religious communities. Methodism, for example, had classes and bands where people shared their lives. Quakers had group examinations, where people reflected together on one another's faithfulness. The anabaptist groups like Brethren, Amish, and Mennonite have proclaimed the caring community as central to faith.

Examples of intensive faith-sharing groups can be found in many congregations. Young parents' support groups, groups for those facing loss and grief, self-help groups, and intensive Bible studies like "Disciple" or "Kerygma" are examples. Each week, most members of Korean-American congregations gather in class meetings to study the faith, to share the events of their lives, and, in prayer, to explore how to live.

Stephen Schmidt, a Lutheran educator, tells the story of one church that instituted a chronic-illness group. All the people in the group shared meanings of chronic illness; special stresses were part of everyday life. There were times of intense anger, and even resentment toward God, when they would ask, "Why did this happen to me?" Moreover, there were times of depression, when an activity that at one time brought joy had to be avoided. The members of the group knew that "persistent stress [pain and illness] wears people down, saps energy and hope, and often leads to depression and gloom."[13] Yet, there were also times of great love and joy.

The community they formed at Grace Church was a feisty, loving group of folks, who walked into the depths together and cried out to God. They were honest about their fragility and their actions that injured others. They affirmed God as a divine companion who suffered alongside them. Their sharing of love brought hope and grace.

The chronic-illness group has been meeting for more than five years. The first meetings were tense and awkward. The illnesses were different: cancer, Lou Gehrig's disease, Crohn's disease, depression, alcoholism. What they shared was a commitment to Christian faith. While their explicit purpose was to explore how faith is a resource for illness, they soon learned the importance of sharing experiences. Meanings flowed only as they seriously encountered one another's needs and feelings.

A structure emerged for the meetings: prayer, sharing of experiences, a time of reflection/encouragement/ challenge, and a closing blessing. Spouses joined the group. The group became yeast for the congregation. In fact, people who were not chronically ill asked if they could participate in a group. In sharing groups like this, we find profound clues about religious learning. Schmidt asserts, "Were a congregation to pattern its own ministry after the experiences of the group . . . churches would be places of shared experiences."[14]

This chronic-illness group exhibited *hospitality, interpretation*, and *practiced presence*. First, the members honored life questions. They learned that ministry occurs as people live together in radical mutuality. Each person was a teacher/learner, engaging in ministry, negotiating meanings, stimulating the others' ethical/theological reflection, interpreting the tradition, and engaging in spiritual growth. They were interpreters among interpreters.

> We make meaning out of stories, and remembering is the only way we have to learn from the past. So almost like psychotherapy, we remember and rehearse that memory or hear it from another, and somehow we are better able to cope with the next day. Someone else shares our story, someone lives in our reality, so we are not alone. So what does the person who is chronically ill do to help another sufferer? Nothing much, except tell stories—which helps *very* much.[15]

Second, this group was a place where the faith tradition and quests for meaning intersected. Illness profoundly challenged meanings. New ones had to be constructed. The faith tradition provided a lens through which the people explored and understood experience. They engaged in theological reflection as they asked fundamental questions about life, death, illness, and suffering. As Schmidt maintains, "Our theology is hardly bookish. . . . It is a theology of experience."[16]

Third, this group became church. Ministry was a gift of shared community, where Christ is embodied. Their life together embodied a hospitable and just space. Their experience in the chronic-illness group changed the participants' views of church: A place without a "hierarchy of ministries," where each person shared individual gifts with the total community.

"Such a congregation would reenvision the Lord's Supper, seeing for maybe the first time that 'real presence' had little to do with changes in bread and wine, but

everything to do with changes in persons."[17] Intensive
sharing groups can become new spaces that challenge the
ordinary, ho-hum character of church. People can learn
that church is a reality of meaning, care, and justice. They
can encounter the sacraments as windows on God's grace,
connecting their experiences of wholeness with God's
presence.

Identify small groups in your experience that could be
intersections for learning. What brought each group
together? What are their purposes? What factors make
them settings for learning? What changes could
enhance the learning process in those groups?

Remaking the Church

The church can be a place to encounter God's presence;
it can be a place of justice, care, and healing for the
world—a place of "real" presence. Yet, the church often
fails to be the Body of Christ; many churches do not heal,
and others lack passion for God and the world. Priorities,
taboos, conflicts, selfishness—all become obstacles to God.
As grace is experienced in *glimpses* of hope and possibility,
so too the church is experienced in glimpses of embodied
love, justice, and care. The church can be a place to
practice the presence of God in the midst of life
experience.

People learn through the communities in which they
participate. Every community holds a meaning-perspective, a faith, that is proclaimed again and again as people
participate in its life. The power of community is apparent

if you live in another culture for any period of time. You may have learned the language in your schoolroom, but it seems different when spoken on the streets. Expectations and rituals of daily contact are also different. You have to be careful not to offend. Cultures are learned by participating in them.

A metaphor to help people understand the power of the church and its ambiguous character is *The Necessary Illusion* by Malcolm Warford, a theological educator. The hope that the church can be the Body of Christ may be illusory, for the church is never adequate, yet it is the only institution focused on the vision of God's in-breaking grace.[18] The church is necessary.

Christian education is as much about seeking to influence the life of the church, the primary environment of Christian learning, as it is about sharing faith with individuals. We learn to be faithful as we participate in the practices of the church. Christian educator Craig Dykstra asks, "What difference does it make that the *church* does Christian education? . . . Christian education is that particular work which the church does to teach the historical, communal, difficult, countercultural practices of the church so that the church may learn to participate in them ever more fully and deeply."[19]

Prayer, Bible reading, worship, study, support and challenge in community, and work for justice—all are means of practicing the presence of God, of shaping the community and persons.

The church is central to Christian meaning-making. Meaning *re-presents* reality. The church itself seeks to live the meanings of the Christian faith and assist people at the intersections of faith and life. Meaning *constructs*. Our identity is affected as we engage the core values and practices offered by the church. Meaning *evokes* powerful commitments and feelings. The church grounds us in a community of identity and passion. Finally, meaning *directs* us into vocation. The call to the church is to live toward wholeness. Theology provides a means for us to clarify how the church itself provides a hospitable and just setting for encountering God's presence.

The church must always be open to the claims of the reign of God—a reign in which God seeks to reverse the order of brokenness and offer shalom, wholeness, hospitality, community, and health. Three concepts are central to the theology of the church. The church is first an "earthen vessel."[20] The church is limited and broken. The church is incarnated in a particular place, with particular characteristics of ethnicity and history. It is a living community, where people seek to respond with integrity to the call of God.

Second, the church is a redemptive community, a place where lives are being made new. Religion is lived in light of eternity. God calls us into justice, harmony, and care for one another and the cosmos. The church is always re-forming. While it is embodied in a particular time and place and remembers and tells a particular story, the church and its story are always open to the call of God to be more faithful. To be a redeeming community, even the practices of the church are open to reformation as they intersect with the experiences of people and the lively presence of God.

Third, the church is sacramental. Through its life, one has a window to the Holy. In the life of the church, we are reminded of the primal events of Christian meaning— that is, the life and resurrection of Jesus, the miracle of God's gracious call of a people, the redemption of God offered in the Exodus, and the creation of the church as the Body of Christ. The activities of the church can point to the presence of God in the world, calling for shalom.

Through education, the church is challenged to embody the presence that redeems and renews life. Each time committees develop programs, they are engaged in educational moments of making meaning and assessing faithfulness. However, the church's faithfulness is always undergirded by God's grace. The church becomes community in its best sense when people make substantial commitments to a group. The intensive Bible-study groups such as "Kerygma" and "Disciple" require commitment to reading, class attendance, and discussion. In the context of commitment, people come to care for and about one another. They experience God's grace among them. Through the life of the church, we glimpse the call of God. Some moments break through aloneness to connection: When another's feelings claim our attention; when we discover that our struggle to listen is also an opportunity to communicate, be challenged, and understood; when we search for support amidst the great crises of life; and where we learn to risk, even when we are not sure of the consequences. The gift of the church is to be a community open to the call and presence of God.

The education of Christians requires participation in the struggle to discern life in light of the incarnation of God, by remembering, loving, telling, and retelling life's story in light of God. Christians are therefore called to live and honor life questions (e.g., in Sunday school and committee meetings), share in the primal events of the faith (worship), care for others on the journey (pastoral care), and call one another into ministry in real life situations (proclamation and action)—to incarnate God's love. Working to enhance the church as an environment of Christian learning is central to the task of Christian education.

Hospitality, Interpretation, and Presence

How do we provide spaces where people can gather together to explore life and share meanings, in light of the faith tradition and the lively presence of God? Contexts for education include worship, preaching, small groups, counseling, music, action projects, decision-making groups. Each local congregation will find particular ways to enable learning through education and ministry. The task is to explore the life of the congregation and to assess it in light of the concepts of hospitable space, practicing presence, intersection, and empowering people to interpret their identity and vocation with faithfulness.

In one congregation, a group of people were revitalized as they sought to connect their congregation's life to another church in the Caribbean. The interrelationship began through a work trip, when parishioners assisted in the development and staffing of an AIDS hostel. In their work together, the people from two cultures learned of each other's commitments to faith.

The mission project enabled them to experience the embodied, redemptive, and sacramental possibilities of the church. First, members of the congregations agreed to remember one another. Sunday announcements included the life and ministry of people in the sister congregation. Second, others agreed to study and pray together across the distance, using common Bible readings. Insights were shared by letter and videotape. Finally, they agreed to send people to each other for work projects. Each of these settings became intentional contexts for learning. Sharing their lives provided an occasion to reflect on the intersection of culture, personal experience, and religion, and to be open to opportunities for ministry. People learned as the churches responded to the loving, transforming presence of God.

CHAPTER SIX

CONVERSING AT THE WALL

Educating in Church and World

Carol was hired as minister to children and youth at Second Church. She was to supervise the church's nursery school, coordinate the youth program, and administer Sunday school for children and youth. The church seemed stable. Youth groups were active. Sunday school was growing slightly as younger families joined the church. The nursery school had a waiting list.

Second Church was a medium-sized congregation in a city of two hundred thousand. The community around the church was not as desirable as it once had been. The local high school was experiencing, for the first time, a drug problem. Its academic ranking had slipped. The city was in transition: a major factory had closed, tax revenues were down, and newer suburbs were draining energy.

During Carol's first months, she met with families in the congregation, young people in schools, and community leaders. She became convinced that, beneath the congregation's surface stability, lay anxiety. Older members were concerned about the neighborhood. Younger members were stretched by long working hours. Community leaders worried about providing adequate city services. School teachers related declining parental involvement

and increased classroom difficulties. Children expressed
fears and pressures.

As a result of her conversations, Carol proposed a major
revision in her job description—half-time in the church
and half-time as a community advocate. She argued that
the church was ministering to only a small part of
children's lives. Ministry to children meant listening to
children, seeking to affect the environment in which they
and their families lived and learned, and reaching out to
those who felt excluded from the church. Carol called on
the church to widen the boundaries of *church* education.

Each person's faith is formed in the intersection of
influential forces: school, job, friends, family, media,
church, volunteer groups, culture. In all these areas,
people deal with ultimate questions. While religious
institutions are the explicit settings in U.S. society for
religious reflection and worship, too often they have
become insulated from experiences in the rest of people's
lives.[1] Religion is thus separated from public life and
relegated to a private sphere, dealing with personal crises
and personal meanings.

The Privatization of Religion

Individualism has profoundly affected the United
States. In *Habits of the Heart,* Robert Bellah and his
colleagues find that commitment to the common good is
fading. They seek to reconnect people. Individual rights
"must be balanced by a renewal of commitment and
community. . . . Such a renewal is indeed a world waiting
to be born, if we only had the courage to see it."[2]
Individualism has freed people from older restrictive and
limiting traditions; yet at the same time, individualism has
separated people from one another. Community is lost,

and people are confused about how to affect public
decisions.

Religion, for generations, has been central to the
definition of U.S. culture. Religious institutions have been
mediating, bridging private and public life and enabling
each to influence the other.[3] In fact, the church has been
called the soul of the nation, providing visions and
resources for public life.[4] Yet, religion has become
privatized, concerned with individualism rather than the
public good.

To illustrate religious individualism, the authors of
Habits of the Heart share an interview with Sheila, a young
nurse: "I believe in God. I'm not a religious fanatic. I can't
remember the last time I went to church. My faith has
carried me a long way. It's Sheilaism. Just my own little
voice."[5] In her case, as in many others, how *my* life is made
meaningful and comfortable is the issue. Sheila accepts
responsibility for *her* views; the problem is that she, like
many others, does not see the need for community or the
need for power to affect public life. She is alone.

The trend toward privatism is further illustrated by two
international anthropologists, Surajit Sinha and Hervé
Varenne, who studied a typical midwestern town. On the
surface, people claim their concern for public life. Each
week, for example, in the local newspaper, a full-page
advertisement is sponsored by local businesses, highlight-
ing Christian religious services. However, the anthropologists discovered that the U.S. values of individualism,
competition, and volunteerism were more determinative
of people's actions than were the values of the churches.[6]

Privatism can devastate both culture and religion. We
separate into our private worlds. Ultimate questions
become focused on *my* life, rather than on the life of the
world. Dealing with meaning and value separately, we

reinforce the brokenness of our world by ignoring our responsibility for, and connectedness to, life itself.

> Privatism placed religion, together with the family, in a compartmentalized sphere that provided loving support but could no longer challenge the dominance of utilitarian values in society at large. Indeed, to the extent that privatization succeeded, religion was in danger of becoming, like the family, "a haven in a heartless world," but one that did more to reinforce the world, by caring for its casualties, than to challenge its assumptions.[7]

While particular issues do stimulate moral outrage, the tenor of daily life expects religion to be a support for individual pain, rather than a vision for building the world. Yet, religions are about both *caring for the wounded* and *providing visions for public discourse*. We have forgotten the latter. Religions are about how people are to live and the kind of world that is to be built.

The argument of this book is that meanings are ultimately personal. No one but me lives in my skin. However, *personal* does not mean *private*. Living at the intersection is very public. Multiple forces of life meet in the intersections. In education we seek to provide hospitable and just spaces, where our lives can be opened for reflection and decision. *Religious* education creates contexts where learning toward wholeness and vocation takes place.

The Goals of Education

Education transcends schools. Education includes the many ways people share and revive their culture as they move into the future. Historian Lawrence Cremin challenges us to think comprehensively, relationally, and publicly about education.

Thinking *comprehensively* means considering the breadth of institutions that have educative dimensions: families, classrooms, museums, businesses, media, government.[8] Corporations, for example, provide preservice and inservice training for employees. People learn the procedures and values of the corporation, specific job tasks, and even human-relations and planning skills. A church executive who attended a workshop for CEOs of major corporations relates that the topics sounded strangely like church: building and enhancing community, honoring values in decision-making, and even "spirituality"—that is, finding a renewing source beyond oneself. A concern about opening international markets has also led several companies to teach languages and cross-cultural communication to their employees.[9]

Education is also *relational.* Educational content and procedures in one agency may be "complementary or contradictory, consonant or dissonant" with each other.[10] Carol knew the interrelation of educational agencies when she proposed that her job at Second Church include time for child advocacy. Carol thought comprehensively: The church is only one institution, affecting only part of the children's lives. Carol thought relationally: To affect the lives of children, the church needs to attend to the interrelationship of educational agencies.

The interrelation of educational agencies is dynamic, like an ecology, involving conflict and support among the agencies. For example, the values some of us learned in churches were reinforced each day as our families nurtured us. Moreover, in some communities, the values taught in the church were directly influenced by local values. The meanings taught by parents, pastors, Sunday school teachers, public-school teachers, and co-workers proceeded in similar directions. For example, Jack remembers that his Sunday school teacher, a family friend, was also his second-grade teacher. Church, school, and family were intimately connected.

Sometimes educational agencies are in conflict. Amish families, for example, first found themselves in conflict with public education in the 1920s, when small, neighborhood-controlled schools were consolidated into larger school systems.[11] In the new schools, Amish children were caught between the values of the school and their peers from the wider community, and their Amish parents. The same was true for Catholics. As public schools emerged, they took on a decidedly Protestant cast, even requiring the reading of the Protestant translation of the Bible.[12] For Catholic parents, schools were in conflict with their religious values.

Finally, Cremin argues that we need to think *publicly* about education. Education is any act in which a person intentionally seeks to learn something or teach someone else. Education is therefore always both public and political. The fundamental values and skills necessary for a people's existence are being defined. To call education *public* means that we need to converse about the values taught and the settings in which teaching occurs.

One example is the current controversy in public schools over the teaching of children in their native languages. The English-only proponents argue that the U.S. is an English-speaking society. Their opponents respond that ethnic children are at risk in schools in which their languages and cultures are not honored. Both reflect deeply held values. The decision about the content of education is public and political. Otherwise, values will be imposed, and the people affected will be unable to participate in the construction of society's values.

What is one value being argued in your school system? What is one in your church? List some values you think are crucial. What, in your meaning-perspective, supports the list you have just made?

Another example is the seminary curriculum. Each seminary curriculum is affected by the faculty's image of a good church leader, by the commitments of academic disciplines (e.g., Bible, history, ethics, theology, education), by the course choices and evaluations of students, and by the churches that seek graduates. Conflict about priorities sometimes emerges when church executives demand the teaching of a particular skill, while professors expect another. The seminary community must adjudicate among competing interests for students' limited time in a degree program.

Curriculum is a *public* document which teaches a particular content. Schools also teach by what they leave out (the null curriculum).[13] For example, one of us taught at a seminary that did not require courses in preaching. Church leaders complained that the lack of such a requirement communicated that preaching was not central to ministry. In fact, at that seminary, counseling was more central to the definition of *minister*.

Churches teach explicitly through their lives; churches also teach by what they ignore. If, for example, churches always use masculine language, they teach exclusion. If churches never mention child abuse in classes, worship, or prayer, they teach by omission that abuse is not the church's concern.

Education is public because we need to decide what is

taught and how it will be taught. Education is political. People use power to influence the aims and processes of the group; they decide what of the past is important and what kind of future they want to create. In a poetic vein, Cremin borrows from philosophers John Dewey and Alfred North Whitehead: "The function of the educator, once again, is prophecy, or the artistic linking of tradition and aspiration."[14] Education stands at the intersection of the past of a people and their hopes. It is "holy ground," where commitments and visions are linked and expressed to others. It is "holy" because education embodies the most sacred, the ultimate values of a people. Without education, a people would not continue into the next generation.

Thus Cremin's definition: Education is "the deliberate, systematic, and sustained effort to transmit, evoke, or acquire knowledge, attitudes, values, skills, or sensibilities, as well as any outcomes of that effort."[15] Education is an intentional process by which people decide what is important to know *and* how they will acquire the knowledge, values, and content to live into the future (curriculum).[16] Education is a context through which people learn their identities and vocations.

Defining Religious Education

In biblical times, Israel was situated between great nations which fought one another for power. This small kingdom with limited resources was buffeted between Assyrians, Egyptians, Babylonians, Greeks, and Romans. A story of the conflict is told in II Kings 18–19, when the Assyrian army surrounds Jerusalem and demands surrender. As the Assyrian representative proclaims his terms, the negotiator from Judah requests that he speak in Aramaic, the language of diplomacy, rather than in

Hebrew, so the people would not hear the dire terms of surrender. Yet, in arrogance, the negotiator refuses and challenges the people. However, inside the city wall, the Hebrews pray in their own language, reminding one another of their God, of God's power, and of the Hebrew traditions. In this story, God's intervention saves the city.

Walter Brueggemann, a biblical scholar, uses this story to illustrate that people of faith must be *bilingual*: "They must have a *public* language for negotiation at the wall. And they must have a more *communal language* for use behind the gate."[17] Brueggemann's metaphors contribute to the conversation about public and private.

As we have pointed out, all events are interpreted. Each of us, alone and in community, seeks to make meaning of experience. The same was true of King Hezekiah and the prophet Isaiah, as they faced the forces of King Sennacherib of Assyria. However, every interpretation depends upon the meaning-perspective of the person or group. Each event is interpreted from a particular point of view.

Living in the Intersection: At the Wall and Behind the Wall

Since religious education occurs at the intersection, it looks both ways, toward the faith community and toward the world. Religious educators, like any educators, are concerned about transmitting their heritage to the next generation and helping members acquire the resources to move into the future. Behind the wall, in churches and synagogues and temples, the creeds, codes, cultic rituals, and patterns of community life are taught. These practices communicate the identities and vocations of the religion. They express meaning-perspectives around which to organize lives.

But religious people also believe that their meanings affect the world, are ultimately significant. Religions have the responsibility to share their ultimate meanings as the public world is built. Therefore, Christian religious education teaches Christians at least to be bilingual, to speak the language of the faith community and also the common languages of public communication.

The concept of intersection further enlarges the notions of "at" and "behind" the wall. The wall is not an impenetrable fortress. The wall is more like the wall of a cell in the body. The cell includes the nucleus and the structures to feed and protect the cell (behind the wall), but the wall itself is permeable. By osmosis, nutrients come in and waste products leave. Ideas cross the wall in both directions. When people come to church, they bring a self that is shaped by the influences at their intersections.

In fact, conversations at the wall are among multiple groups, each of which has its own distinct conversation behind its wall. We live in diverse communities. Anne, a teenager, has friends who are Christians, Jews, Muslims, Hindus, and Buddhists. Whenever her group talks about their future and issues that face them, they are talking "at the wall," among their various religious traditions. Each is profoundly affected by the conversation. Ideas and practices flow back and forth. No youth in this group can enter his or her church, temple, or synagogue without bringing the shared conversations.

Moreover, the group is also ethnically diverse; it includes people from Korean, Japanese, Brazilian, Indian, Slovakian, and Chinese cultures, as well as European-Americans. Each person's meaning-perspective is influenced by ethnic perspectives, by religious perspectives, and by their interaction.

Education is comprehensive, relational, and public. Living in a pluralistic world, like the U.S., requires people to know their faith, live their vocation in the public world, *and* communicate that faith with integrity to others, as they interact and decide how to live together. In a plural world, our temples of meaning touch. If we are to live with one another and communicate our deepest commitments to one another, both our education and our religious education need to be public.

Yet, the privatization of religion has caused us to fail in both commitments. Churches have failed to address adequately the formation of the language behind the wall. As Brueggemann says, "The story which has lost power is the one behind the walls. We end up . . . without the will, courage, energy or self-knowledge to act."[18] Churches fail to educate for vocation. If we believe our faith is crucial for the future of the world, Christian religious education needs to communicate that faith and help people connect it to living.

Privatism has also caused us to fail to reach out adequately to others at the wall. To be just, the participants in the conversation at the wall must strive to hear one another, as theologian Henry Young argues:

> When we fail to allow things within nature to disclose themselves to us, we force them to become what we want them to be rather than what their inherent value suggests. . . . Only when we recognize this fact can we learn to respond to all phenomena—human and nonhuman—without coercing reality into conformity with our biases.[19]

Each perspective is known, criticized, and expanded as a result of the interaction. Sometimes the conversation leads to unity; at other times, to conflict. We need to learn how to engage openly and mutually in the conversation.

Educating Christians in a public, plural world means teaching that faith is related to the world, and helping people communicate across differences by building coalitions of care and justice. Only by being public do we affirm that our faith matters. By being public, we can be open to the power of God to call us, listen to others in mutuality, and move into a future with new possibilities.

Name an issue that is important to you. In a paragraph, describe that issue, using the language of the people within the wall. Then discuss the same issue, using the languages at the wall.

Christian Religious Education

Christian education is about forming faith—that is, about the basic meaning-perspectives through which a person views reality. Faith formation means that the perspectives of Christian faith become a lens through which persons view the world. For example, children are immersed in the stories, concepts, and images of the faith, and so they have a repertoire of meanings with which to interpret life experiences.

Alice, whom we met at the annual church celebration, was influenced by the practice of the Eucharist (chapter 5). As she learned to lift the broken bread to God, her meaning-perspective, her faith, was being formed. She learned that God was intimately present to the world. Similarly, Jennifer learned about prayer at her church (chapter 3). When her grandfather died, she experienced both the limits of prayer and the power of God. Her meaning-perspective included God's presence, but she also learned that she needed to reinterpret the meaning of prayer.

As this last example suggests, Christian education is also about faith transformation, the dynamic process of *reinterpreting* both life experience and one's meaning-perspectives. Religions themselves are about ultimate questions, the fundamental conditions under which we live. Education opens us to transformation. For Jennifer, God's presence became more than "answers" to problems. The little boy whose father died in the mine accident was asking about (and changing) his view of God as he considered the fairness of the mine owners.

The education of Christians involves much more than content (meaning-schemes). Meaning-perspectives also are formed and transformed. Three goals for education address the aims of formation and transformation: (1) explore at the intersection; (2) practice theological reflection; and (3) call to vocation.

First, to explore at the intersection requires that people both acquire key elements of the Christian story and vision, and learn to be self-reflective about their experiences. People need to know the Christian story in order to refract experience through it. Religions usually have four elements: a creed, a code, a cultus, and a community (chapter 3). Each of these elements can communicate the Christian faith.

Through creed, one learns key stories, concepts, images, and symbols. Behind the wall, the Hebrews remembered the stories and prayers of God's deliverance. Through code, one learns the practices expected of a Christian in encountering others in the world. For example, the image "children of God" teaches us to treat others as we would want to be treated, because we are all God's heirs. Cultus teaches through the practices of ritual and worship: Postures used in prayer teach our relationship to God; to kneel at communion shows our dependence upon God. Finally, the community teaches as we participate in its life. The community is "the necessary illusion," a faulted institution seeking to live faithfully.

However, also at the intersection is life experience. Carol knew the power of the community to "shape" children. The town was in transition, and children were fearful. Their schools were becoming places of threat. She became convinced that the church needed to help children address their experiences. Also, the young people at Bethel Church, because of the after-school program, reflected on and addressed their life in the neighborhood (chapter 5). They painted a mural, under the tutelage of teachers who knew the neighborhood, to show how the society was seeking to influence them. The first goal of Christian religious education is to encounter and explore at the intersection.

Second, Christian education assists people to practice theological reflection. More than knowing the forces that influence us at the intersection and those resources we can call on, we need a way to reflect theologically and make decisions. Four sources for theological reflection used by many people are scripture, tradition, reason, and experience.[20] People make decisions about their meaning-schemes through consideration of these sources.

In the text, four sources for theological reflection are identified. What would you add? Which of the sources is most important for you? How does this source influence your decisions?

Theological reflection does not merely employ concepts. We also draw on the wealth of images and stories in our repertoires. As Andrew Greeley has clarified, religious imagination is a powerful source for theological reflection. Holy week is filled with vivid images of betrayal, suffering, crucifixion, and new life, which powerfully inform our theologies. When we encounter experience, we draw on our stories, concepts, and images, to make meaning.[21]

Theological reflection involves critical reflection because faith is always in process, old meanings are renewed and reshaped. The chronic-illness group, for example, engaged in theological reflection as the people sought to understand their experiences of illness (chapter 5). Both the Christian tradition and their experiences were enriched in the encounter.

Finally, Christian religious education *calls people into vocation*. As theologian David Tracy says, theology reveals meanings that can "transform all human lives in some recognizable personal, social, political, ethical, cultural, or religious manner."[22] Christian religious education does not end with reflection. Reflection leads us into action. Mildred, for example, embodied the call to justice in her interactions with people. Adrienne considered changing her career because of her encounter with God (chapter 1). Parker Palmer's image for action is co-creation.[23] As people create, they, in turn, are created by the world. They are called into vocation, living toward wholeness.

Toward Vocation

Carol called Second Church to expand its vision of church education. Children were "shaped" in the community. A church education that ignored the community ignored significant influences at the intersection. Christian religious education occurs in the church and reaches out to help people face the world. Christian religious education also occurs in the world itself, as people encounter the ultimate dimensions of life.

From the Church to the World

Helen was recruited as teacher of the fourth-grade Sunday school class. She was employed at a local public school. During the school year, a child in her class was physically abused at home. Helen worked with her school colleagues to care for the child and to confront the abuser. As a result of this experience, Helen was appointed to head a task force to prepare a school curriculum on physical and sexual abuse.

Because of her faith, Helen believed that the church had resources to address abuse, resources that dealt holistically with the child, family, and community. As she worked with her school, Helen also asked her church whether she and Ardis, a social worker in the congregation, might teach a six-week series on sexual and physical abuse for elementary children and their parents. The request stimulated much conversation within the church. Some people were not sure the church should speak on such a volatile issue. After two members shared their own experiences with abuse, the series was approved.

A committee was appointed to assist with the study. As they worked, they discovered that the church's theology was a significant resource. The concepts of child of God and shalom, as well as the Bible's advocacy for the weak (the orphan, widow, and stranger), provided new perspectives on the issue. Through the study, many in the congregation opened their eyes to the abuse around them. The church agreed to support a local shelter.

Helen and Ardis became resource people to the community as children's education expanded through the schools, and parents' education expanded through the mental-health center. In the school, Helen and Ardis could not use the language behind the wall—the language of the church—but their ideas and language at the wall, in the public forum, were significantly influenced by the church. The educating of church members through the Sunday school became an impetus to community education. Church education led members into the world to affect public life.

From the World to the Church

Oftentimes, religious learning occurs beyond the walls of the church. Margaret Ann attended a speech given by former President Jimmy Carter. For many in the audience, religious learning occurred as people heard him speak about volunteerism. People packed the auditorium, coming early to get seats. He was met by a standing ovation, warm and enthusiastic. People were excited to hear him.

He talked of the agenda of the Carter Center, a nonprofit organization which searches "the world to look for what others aren't doing." For instance, the Center discovered that many children of the world are not being vaccinated against common childhood diseases. Part of the reason is competition among the organizations which provide services for child health. The Center took on the challenge. Carter reported that while only 20 percent of the world's children were immunized six years ago, more than 80 percent are today.

"We stopped the war for three days in El Salvador to immunize children. There's a hunger there for assistance and care and education."[24] People at the lecture caught a vision of how much can be done about public issues when a group such as the Carter Center mobilizes energy. The enthusiasm of the crowd was contagious; the diversity of the crowd was encouraging.

While Carter spoke primarily in the language of national politics, a language at the wall, he also spoke in the language of his Baptist faith community. Many Protestants in the audience knew he was talking of the example of Christ and our calling to care for our neighbor. During a meeting of a Bible-study group just a few days later, a discussion of Jeremiah prompted a listing of modern-day prophets, and several people mentioned Carter. The religious learnings from the Carter speech returned behind the walls of the community of faith and influenced the members' understandings of vocation afresh, as they recommitted to support the local chapter of Habitat for Humanity.

Carter's speech prompted religious learning in the public. People in the audience connected their actions as volunteers with their commitments to public life and to their faith. The Carter Center itself represented a public organization which, because of the faith of its founder, crosses the wall that connects religious faith and public life. In this particular situation, a public occasion for religious learning became also an opportunity for the church to educate about the public vocation of its members.

Opportunities for religious learning and teaching abound within the public world. Movies, plays, political campaigns, and public forums—all are occasions through which people are confronted by ultimate questions. For example, Skokie, Illinois, has erected a monument to remember the victims of the Holocaust and to honor the freedom fighters who resisted the Nazi imprisonment of Jews. The monument prompts religious learning which addresses the pathos and injustice of the Holocaust as well as the determination and courage of those who stand for freedom. The monument reminds religious groups about living together as a diverse people. It also becomes a backdrop for efforts of church and synagogue leaders to communicate about issues of justice and to work to resettle victims of political abuse.

> Where have you experienced a public occasion that was profoundly religious? Describe the experience.

In those examples, the impetus for religious education came from both the church and the community. Religious faith was not private. The intersection of faith and life was addressed, as were people's meanings and vocations. Education that engages life honors our belief that God participates with us—we are co-creators in loving and transforming the world. Carol is right. The church must engage life experience. The belief that religion is of ultimate significance and that God is involved in life calls us to education that is comprehensive, relational, and public.

PART THREE

CHRISTIAN EDUCATION

CHAPTER SEVEN

INTERPRETING AMONG INTERPRETERS

Teaching

The nine seventh- and eighth-graders were finishing a study about God for their confirmation class. Animatedly, they talked about the creed they were writing for next week's worship service. Aaron, the wisecracker, was unusually quiet. Several young people shared ideas: God is creator, God is love, God is a friend.

One of the boys prodded, "Ask Aaron. Ask Aaron. He has a neat idea." Aaron seemed embarrassed.

"Aaron, do you want to share?" the teacher asked.

Quietly, Aaron answered, "O.K.," and slowly started to speak: "God has such a big job. God has to care for all of us and we're not easy. God is all alone." He paused. "I guess God is a single parent."

The class and the teacher were quieted; the kidding ended. Heads nodded in affirmation.

Jean said, "Let's use that next week."

Heather added, "It must be tough to be all alone." And the group set to work, constructing their creed. Prominent in it was the image of God as single parent.

For six months, the class had explored some of the major themes of the Bible and heroes of the faith. This unit was about the ways teenagers think about God (theological method). In the first session, they had

examined biblical images for God. They discussed texts
about God as friend, father, judge, Savior, liberator, and
mother hen. Through the second week, they talked to
family and friends about their views of God. On Sunday
they shared ideas: God is like my grandpa who always is
strong; God is energy; God is everywhere and in all of us;
God is love. The third week, they explored creeds
(Apostles' Creed, the Westminster Confession of Faith,
the Korean Creed). During the last week, they put all the
images and concepts they had affirmed into a creed for
worship. In this rich environment, the image of God as a
single parent became powerful for them.

Teachers and students worked together, learning from
each other. The space was hospitable. The method
encouraged them to listen to themselves, one another,
friends, family, and classic documents of the tradition.
Together, they stood in the intersection—each person
bringing experiences that were considered in light of the
Christian story. In the end, they made a decision: The
image of God as single parent, alone and responsible,
became part of their meanings.

Learning is unique to each individual. A classroom,
sanctuary, or any other setting becomes educative only
when learning occurs—when a learner makes or discovers
meaning. Meanings are personal because they depend on
the unique interaction of life experience, meaning-
perspectives, meaning-schemes, and the communities that
influence us. Therefore, meanings will not be uniform for
everyone, even in the same context. Each learner connects
with a particular set of experiences.

Among any worshiping congregation, for instance, are
persons who uncritically experience a liturgy; it resonates
with meanings already in place. Others in the congregation are challenged by a word or phrase. New ideas may
cause them to explore their views and reconstruct

personal theologies. And a few may find that the liturgy speaks to them of God's love so powerfully that their hearts are strangely warmed, leaving them freshly energized or transformed.

The members of the confirmation class responded to the image of God as a single parent, according to personal experiences of single parents. Aaron, who first observed that God is alone, has a good friend who lives with one parent. His experience of that home enabled him to empathize with God who, he realized, has no peer or mate. Aaron learned about God by drawing on his own experiences, as well as those of the religious community, and therefore, he learned uniquely. His idea became part of the intersection for the others. Each youth made connections with meanings that were brought into the intersection and emerged with altered meanings.

Teachers as Co-learners

The uniqueness of learners does not, however, render the teacher irrelevant. The teacher is an interpreter among interpreters. The teaching role affords an opportunity to guide a gathered group. The learning environment can be ordered so that a group is either controlled by the teacher's meanings or freed to explore alternate meanings together. Teaching always involves power, as aims and processes are defined.

We have all experienced "school" where the teacher is the authority. We are so conditioned to that paradigm that whenever we enter a situation that resembles a school, we automatically look to the teacher to set the rules. Teachers have power. Teaching takes place in a context of power—the commitments of a school board or the values expected by a community. Meanings which threaten dominant power are often ignored. For instance, students in the former Soviet Union were taught that communism brought a fair and satisfying way of life, while students in the United States were taught that capitalism brought a fair and satisfying way of life. Little opportunity existed to consider the inadequacies of either. The meanings of the dominant power defined reality.

> Identify the groups in your church and community that influence what is taught. Which groups have the most influence? Why?

Although the teacher's authority sometimes has been misused, that authority also can work positively to set students free to explore ideas and discover personal meanings. The teacher can create a context for mutual learning. A long-range planning committee in one growing church, recognizing that space had become a critical problem, set four options before the congregation. The options ranged from maintaining the status quo to buying new land and building a new church. Following a congregational gathering over lunch, the chair of the committee facilitated discussion of the options. Someone asked him what he thought the church should do.

He answered truthfully, "I really don't know. I'm exploring it along with you." As a co-learner, the chair kept options open. Participants were anxious at first, but eventually gained confidence and entered into the imagining alongside a leader who was also risking. The teacher creates mutuality by approaching education as an open process in which both leader and learner seek to make sense of life.

Mutuality presents the teacher with an opportunity to continue to grow and learn. Just as a preacher delivering a sermon for the second time may discover new meaning in it, the teacher also discovers new meaning while sharing in learning with students. Mary Elizabeth Moore captures this idea in her image "teaching from the heart." When we teach from the heart, we revere "the other—other persons, other cultures, other parts of the environment."[1] By *revering* others' meanings, the teacher becomes a co-learner.

A university professor of medical ethics, whose classes dealt with controversial topics such as abortion and euthanasia, took pride in keeping his convictions a secret. He argued that this gave the students freedom to explore their own stances. However, he did not really revere the students. Withholding his convictions left students guessing at the "right" answer. The professor's power was retained. He refused to be a partner, an interpreter among interpreters.

To be a co-learner, one must listen. Listening is the starting point for hospitable space. Hearing one another involves seeking to enter the meanings of others, for only then can we begin to understand them. Stereotyping, the antithesis of co-learning, prevents us from seeing others fully. We see only one dimension with a label on it. When we listen, we recognize that each individual is unique.

Listening also empowers transformation. The attention paid by a careful listener gives courage and encourages questioning. Often, as we prepared the manuscript of this book, the attention of a co-author enabled one of us to articulate clearly a point of view which previously was only half known. Hearing involves an intuitive and embodied connectedness with another.

Educator Laurent Daloz describes the role of mentor in a similar and poetic manner: "[Mentors] are suffused with magic and play a key part in our transformation. Their purpose . . . is to remind us that we can, indeed, survive the terror of the coming journey and undergo the transformation by moving through, not around, our fear."[2]

When our meanings threaten to shatter or collapse, when our temples of meaning must be reconstructed, we are frightened. We may shore up the defenses around inadequate meaning-perspectives, hoping they will stand. In a hospitable and just space, alongside a co-learner (or mentor), we may find the strength and courage to rebuild our temples. The co-learner who listens and honors our reconstruction project—not manipulating or controlling but supporting alongside—may indeed seem to have the power of magic.

Listening is not passive. The listener must focus and actively follow the train of thought. The active listener enters fully into an argument, seeking to hear the truth of it. At the same time, the active listener hears critically and analytically, reflecting the ideas with fresh words. Marie told how her teacher helped her to form ideas:

> I talked with him in his study one day, speaking with conviction about a paper I was writing but only half knowing what I wanted to say. He took notes as I talked. Occasionally he read back out of the notes. His retelling of my thoughts was a profound "Ah ha!" moment. I clarified and claimed the new meanings which had been coming to birth over many months of research and writing.

The attention of the listener allowed ideas to come to birth. We do "hear into" speech. Listening has impact.

However, a listener's experience of our story is always inadequate. Communication, at best, is partial. I say, "I understand." Yet I do not ever know totally the reality another describes to me. I always connect another's reality with my remembered meanings. The one in the role of student will hear only a fragment of what the one in the role of teacher understands. The teacher hears only a fragment of what the learner offers. Recognizing our limits helps both teacher and student to approach the context for learning with humility.

Not only is our understanding of another's experience fragmentary, but we attend only to a fragment of the reality around us. We are not fully aware of the power of the expectations of the dominant culture to control the meanings we share. Thus, we need one another's perspectives as we explore experience and make meaning. The teacher or leader can be only co-learner. To claim a greater role in the meaning-making of another is to presume too much.

The most compelling reason for the teacher to be a co-learner is that individuals reach their fullest sense of humanity in relationship. Mutuality encourages all participants to learn from one another and honor the meanings that each discovers. The confirmation class honored Aaron's idea of God as a single parent. His image resonated with their own experiences and added a dimension to their understanding of God. Learning in relationship means that each participant, including the one designated teacher, can risk, knowing that others support us on the journey.

Because of research in human development, theories of teaching and learning have emphasized the learner. New theories must equally emphasize the teacher. The teacher's interpretation of what is learned will tell us as much about the teacher as about the students. Tests, for instance, may reveal more about the teacher's meaning-system than about what the students "learned." Teachers can interact more effectively and justly with the students when they recognize their own questions and share their meanings with the students.

Teachers seek to create contexts for learning. Since we know one another's realities only fragmentarily, listening is thus the starting place for teaching. Mutuality and co-learning empower us to enter more deeply into experience and risk.

The Imperative to Teach

Why do we teach? First, we teach to learn and to share our learnings. Teaching provides an opportunity to scan interpretations. Humans are always in process, needing to make sense or discover meaning amidst the happenings of our lives. The story of the two travelers on the road to Emmaus is an example. As the story begins, the travelers are trying to make sense of the crucifixion and resurrection events.

"But we had hoped that he was the one to redeem Israel," they say, indicating that their earlier meaning for Jesus' life had become inadequate (Luke 24:21). Later, as they recognize Jesus at the breaking of bread, they reinterpret.

One says to the other, "Were not our hearts burning within us while he was talking to us on the road, while he was opening the scriptures to us?" (Luke 24:32). They are making sense—scanning possible interpretations—in a new way, reconstructing the story in light of their experience at dinner.[3]

Scanning is a compelling reason for teaching expressed by many Sunday school teachers. They learn as they study and prepare. At first, they often say yes to teaching out of a sense of duty, but they continue to say yes because of their growth. The events of their lives compel them to make or discover meanings, and they do that by committing to co-learning.

In teaching, we also share our learnings. When we make sense of life experiences, we want to express that meaning. In the Emmaus story, the need is imperative: "That same hour they got up and returned to Jerusalem. . . . Then they told what had happened on the road, and how he had been made known to them in the breaking of the bread" (Luke 24:33*a*, 35). Life experience provides both the content and impetus for teaching.

Second, human beings hunger for connectedness. We who write this book find that our jobs often take us away from friends and families. When we return from travel, we take time to share what happened. Even though others cannot know completely what we experienced, we seek to be "heard," if only fragmentarily, by others. Their hearing establishes connection. The connection established in teaching is energizing. To teach is to send forth energy. Learning releases energy which flows back. As Mary Elizabeth Moore discloses, "Teaching from the heart has to do with receiving depleted energy, not to hold onto it or judge it bad, but to send it out again for renewal."[4] A student's growing confidence replenishes the energy spent by the teacher. Released and shared energy funds the joy of learning. To stand alongside while others learn or search for meanings is a joy and privilege.

Third, we teach because we have experienced God's good news. When we encounter the "Holy," we feel compelled to "go tell it on the mountain!" The metaphor of dance is apt: The dance is so joyful that we invite others to dance as well. God is waiting for partnership and calling us to transformation. That transformation is painful. It requires that old meanings die in order for us to find new life (resurrection). The shipwreck metaphor of Sharon Parks depicts the devastation that precedes transforma-

tion. As an old meaning reveals its inadequacy, we are cast
adrift. To face the risk of transformation, caring
mutuality is crucial. Theologian Rita Nakashima Brock
writes of this caring:

> Without a safe and nurturing environment for remember-
> ing, in which we can experience the pain of our own
> distinctive brokenness, be angry, and begin to grieve over
> our brokenheartedness, we remain lost to ourselves and
> each other, cut off from the grace that gives us life.[5]

Because we need healing and because we have experienced God's amazing healing, we seek opportunities to
teach, sharing God's good news with co-learners.

A final motivation for teaching is the search for truth,
wholeness, and justice. That passion gives impulse to a
pilgrimage in which both teacher and students participate.
Parker Palmer writes that "to teach is to create a space in
which obedience to truth may be practiced."[6] We teach,
then, because truth matters so much, because there is
good news to be shared, because we hunger for wholeness,
because learning energizes, and because we need communities within which to search for meaning and vocation.

Creating Contexts for Learning

Teachers seek to create contexts for learning. The
context for learning is an intersection (chapter 4),
bringing together past meanings, the experience and
meanings of the community, present experience, and
visions of the future. The intersection becomes a learning
context when there is hospitable and just space in which
interpreters practice God's presence together.

The Context

Hospitality and justice are dependent upon both seeking
relationships and honoring differences. "No one voice or

single species is the only one that counts," theologian Sallie McFague argues. "One of the principal insights of both feminism and postmodern science is that while everything is interrelated and interdependent, everything (maple leaves, stars, deer, dirt—and not just human beings) is different from everything else."[7]

The learning community is an ecosystem in which each person contributes to the whole. The teacher seeks to empower those in the community to hear and know one another. Control or manipulation is not the aim. Rather, as theologian Henry Young describes, the aim is to enter "into creative dialogue" and participate in the "authenticity" of each participant's efforts at meaning-making.[8] Hospitable and just space enables participants to be more aware, to take into account more fully their whole and authentic selves.

When we honor all parts of the ecosystem, we risk differences of opinion which often cannot be integrated or synthesized. The dissonance and the ambiguity they cause may be painful. Yet we need to learn to live in their midst if we are to incarnate mutuality and build a just learning community.

In the learning context, we engage more than ourselves and others. The *content* of Christian education includes also the great witnesses from the past who have influenced the faith and given it power through time. Even those witnesses were dissonant. They also attempted to understand their experiences in light of their encounter with the Holy. Because experiences are different, their interpretations focused on particular concerns and conclusions. They are partners with us and others as we seek to understand. A context for learning includes witnesses from the past, the demands of others in the world, and our contemporary experiences with God.

Why do you teach? What kind of environment do you want to create for learning? Describe as fully as possible the gifts of hospitality and justice you bring to the ministry of teaching.

Preparing to Teach

Much of the creation of a hospitable and just space depends upon the teacher's preparation before "class" begins. The teacher considers those who will be present in the process. Who might they be? What might be their questions, fears, and anxieties? Even with some idea of the meanings which participants bring into the situation, the teacher as co-learner also expects surprises. "Other participants will have much to teach me," he or she thinks.

The teacher's preparation also includes taking stock of her or his own questions and prejudices. Being able to articulate these as the community begins to form makes the space more just. Earlier we commented on the medical-ethics professor who took pride in keeping his convictions secret. Not only did he refuse to be authentic in community, but he blocked others from sharing their meanings freely in creative dialogue.

List some of the major issues with which your church is struggling. Identify groups that have taken a stand on each issue. Name the values on which they base their stances.

Undergirding learning is the graceful presence of God. Together we seek to be open to God's call. The teacher invites others to practice presence. The teacher both models the practicing of presence and honors the discernment of others.

Even when the teacher has attended to his or her own meanings, taken account of others' meanings and questions, and been open to God, the context of learning will not necessarily be smooth and flowing. Some participants will resist being there. Others will be afraid. Some may block efforts to make the space just. Still others will confront or contradict. When learners participate together with authenticity, resistance is regularly present.

Rather than fearing or avoiding resistance, the co-learning teacher understands and welcomes it. A participant who exhibits resistance is acting out of personal meanings. Resistance provides an opportunity to deal with personal issues and injustices.

During an intensive Bible-study class, one man became angry at the assumption of the curriculum writers that a tithe was mandatory. An authoritarian teacher, operating out of the school paradigm, might have stopped dialogue by pointing out that the writers were theologically trained and that the Bible is the standard for Christians. However, the teacher, operating out of the co-learner paradigm, heard this man's concerns, and the class explored the influences in their intersection for learning.

The man's family finances were burdened by bankruptcy; although he and his wife gave generously of their time and talents, they believed they could not currently tithe financially. God's grace enabled the community to help him shed the paralyzing guilt (resistance) that could drive him from the group. Together, they worked to understand tithing as gift and response to God. A teacher creates contexts for learning by modeling hospitable and just space, by practicing presence, and by acting as an interpreter among other interpreters.

PREPARING TO TEACH

I. Explore the subject matter.

II. Reflect on yourself as teacher.
   A. Identify personal concerns and issues that influence your teaching and reflection.
   B. Consider how you are listening to the meanings of class members.
   C. Consider how you are listening to God's call to wholeness and justice.

III. Reflect on members of the class.
   A. Think about concerns, experiences, and knowledge of class members. Explore their wider world.
   B. Wonder how the content may have been important to them. Think about connections that can be made to their context.

IV. Examine the setting for learning (room arrangement, time of day, materials, etc.). Explore approaches for teaching and decide on the process to engage the class in dialogue and critical reflection. (Realize that mutuality means that plans may be altered in interaction with the class.)

Teaching Skills

The co-learning approach requires listening skills, knowledge of a content area, understanding of human learning (development), facility for group process, recognition of God's grace, sensitivity to oppression, passion for justice, flexibility, empathy, and a desire to grow. All these qualities can be cultivated.

A *good listener* works actively to attend to the speaker. Knowing that we are able to take in only a fragment of any communication causes us to work harder, to use our analytical and critical skills, to absorb as much as possible. We seek to "hear each other into" speech, recognizing our differences and making space for each voice to be heard.

Co-learning asks not less, but more of a teacher. The teacher seeks to *know as much as possible* about the content of faith and experience, and to approach content (what is known) with the tentativeness of one who is eager to learn and relearn. Co-learning focuses on practicing obedience to truth. Content arises from the ways people view their experiences in the world. For instance, the content and perspective of this book, as of any book, are provisional. Each theory of Christian education focuses on certain aspects of experience and ignores others.[9]

Theories of human learning and development have influenced the field of religious education. Curriculum has been written to promote "development." Practitioners have relied upon it to guide them. Misunderstood, these theories can label people and lead to manipulative educational methods. A co-learning teacher studies human development in order to shed light on the differences, helping us to honor and accept people. For example, theories of learning and development offer insights about gender and ethnicity. Some research examines contrasts in the development of men and women. Carol Gilligan uncovers the importance of relationship in women's moral decision-making. Other theories explore differences among ethnic communities. Nathan and Julia Hare look at the rituals of transition that are important for the maturing of African American boys and girls.[10]

The co-learning teacher also studies and *becomes adept at group process*. Knowledge of the ways groups operate and the techniques for including others enriches teaching. A skilled teacher learns to recognize when a group is ready to move on to another subject; when one member is left out; and how to help the group respond to an over-participating member. Co-learning is group learning.

Sensitivity to oppression and passion for justice are crucial. God's call "to do justice, and to love kindness, and to walk humbly with your God" extends to teaching (Micah 6:8*b*). A hospitable and just space is a place to search for truth. Part of creating that space means that we will have *empathy* with others. We seek to understand their questions, support those in pain, and remain open to God's surprising grace. Surprises require us to be *flexible*. We are not in control. The intersection where learning takes place is simply a fleeting space through which we, along with others, are privileged to pass.

Finally, the co-learning teacher desires to grow. A hunger for greater *wholeness* drives us to reach out to others. In community, in relationships that are mutual and loving, we can grow toward that wholeness which is a gift of God's grace.

A Teaching Method

Teaching creates a context in which people meet at the intersections of their lives to explore meaning and vocation. That context is a hospitable and just space, where interpreters work together to practice the presence of God. The teachers of the confirmation class honored the life experience of the students at the same time they engaged the theological tradition. They helped the teenagers make sense of their experiences.

Methods for teaching need to address both the beliefs we articulate *and* our underlying meaning-perspectives. The goal of each teaching session is to empower participants to make decisions about the meanings that shape their lives and the vocations which express those meanings. Christian teaching seeks to help us live faithfully.

Teaching involves mutual reflection among people in a community of faith. One concrete method for teaching as interpreting among interpreters has three central elements: exploring, considering, and discerning.[11]

Teaching as Discernment
Exploring:
Attending to and Remembering
(Experiences, Images, Stories, and Concepts
of self, culture, and faith tradition)

LIFE EXPERIENCE

For the purpose of living holistically
and justly into the world[12]

Considering:
Affirming and Grieving

Discerning:
Naming and Deciding

Through teaching, people are called to critical reflection and response. They are sent on a journey to make
sense of their lives. Even "content" (past meanings,
concepts, images, and experiences, as well as explicit new
ideas, concepts, images, and skills we have learned) is
encountered in relationship to experience. People *explore*
possible meanings as they attend to and remember the
images, stories, and concepts that are resources for their
meanings. We glean our past and the traditions that are
important for us, to collect possible resources for
meaning.

Life experience and "content," filtered together, may
lead us to *considering*. We ask, "What do I do with what I
have discovered? Do I reject it, does it confirm what I
already know, do I integrate it into my beliefs, or do I risk
change?" We weigh, ponder, or seek to solve. Considering
can lead us to affirm the temples of meaning that have
previously grounded us. However, we also may grieve as
we are compelled to give up meanings that have been
central to our self-understanding but are no longer
adequate.

Life experience and "content" may lead also to
discerning how to live in light of the Holy. We ask, "What is
this new meaning? What is expected of me? What am I
called to do?" Learning affects the way we name our
experiences and decide to interact with one another.
Discerning can lead back to considering or exploring.

In life, these three moments are never as distinct as they
appear on a diagram. It is a muddle. We discern, consider,
and explore all at the same time, moving back and forth
among these moments. While classrooms often start with
exploration, providing students with new content to
consider, life experience often begins with decisions and
issues that puzzle us. The interaction among these
moments is dynamic. However, a teaching plan involves

the provision of time for each element within a session and can begin at any of these three moments. While plans may neatly move through each moment, we need to realize that every learner will engage the elements uniquely and dynamically, as new issues are brought to the teaching experience.

Teaching and learning are a means of *critical reflection*, connecting the learner to the images, concepts, and stories at the center of his or her meaning-making.[13] In other words, we can become more and more aware of the layout of our temples and their furnishings, what they look like from the outside, and even what their walls touch in the wider environment. Let's examine this teaching process through three examples, each starting with a different moment. In each example, we see the dynamic interaction of the moments.

Beginning with Exploring

In the confirmation class, the teachers usually began with exploring, each week using different content. Sometimes they began with biblical images, stories, and concepts. On other days they looked at images and concepts in creeds. At still other times, they focused on family experiences.

The day they read scripture passages about God, the teachers provided time to *consider* meanings for the passages they read, to weigh the options they heard. One boy, for example, giggled at the image of "suckling at a breast" as describing the relationship with God. A girl saw the image of mother hen as intriguing. She had visited her grandparents' farm, and the protection she saw a mother hen giving her chicks captured that image. She *affirmed* it. God the Father was one image most of them understood, yet they also *grieved*. They knew that not all people had parents who protected or cared for them. In their conversation, the young people heard new images, compared them to the concepts they already possessed, and struggled to hold new ideas and feelings in tension with old patterns. One boy said that Jesus reveals a lot about God.

The goal of the confirmation class was *discernment,* helping the teenagers to claim the faith and church membership. They were to *name* their beliefs and *decide* which ideas and images they would use in the creed they were writing. The process of exploring, considering, and discerning repeated itself each week.

While they usually began with an *exploring* activity, several sessions later the teachers began with *considering,* as the youngsters looked at the changes that had occurred for them. And the regular task of providing part of the liturgy for the Sunday service called them to *discern.* Because joining the church culminated the study, all their efforts ultimately focused on *discerning* their place in God's creation.

Beginning with Considering

An associate pastor, Ellen, was scheduled to preach in Concord, New Hampshire, the Sunday after the explosion of the space shuttle *Challenger.* Several of the young people in her church went to the school where Christa McAuliffe taught. The people in her congregation and others in the town were proud that one of their own was to be the first civilian in space.

The Sunday after the *Challenger* explosion was a time for *grieving.* Their old meanings of pride had been inappropriate. Ellen knew it was like a funeral. People were seeking to understand. She also knew they were *considering* meanings that had failed them and were searching for explanations that made sense. Meaning-making would take time. All she could do was start a teaching process that would help the people and herself explore options.

The day began with Sunday school. Ellen attended the youth class. They told stories about Christa McAuliffe. They angrily questioned the safety of U.S. space equipment. They cried together because so much did not make sense. Ellen listened, sharing their pain. While she had not known the teacher, she too had participated in the pride of the town and empathized deeply. Ellen did not try to control their insights; she let them share and supported them as they *named* some of the meanings that were being challenged.

Worship began with young people speaking to the congregation of the feelings they had identified in their class. Through song, prayer, scripture reading, and sermon, Ellen led the worshipers to *attend to* the resources of Christianity. She read passages about power, loss, and pain, helping them explore the faith tradition. Her sermon *affirmed* the loss the Hebrews felt in the Exile.

At a moment when people's temples of meaning were shaking, Ellen was present. She taught. The Christian tradition became "content" to be *considered* as people sought to make decisions and *discern* meanings. Ellen was sensitive to their pain and explicitly addressed it. One parishioner said, "Her questions were our questions." While the case of the *Challenger* disaster is dramatic, the teaching began in the context of people's *considering*, *affirming*, and *grieving*.

Another teaching experience that began with *considering* occurred in a Bible class where people were struggling with historical criticism. One person put it poignantly: "If all these events aren't facts, then how do I know what to believe?" The pastor, an empathetic teacher, addressed the anxiety about challenged meanings. Rather than piling on more information, he knew the people needed to *consider* and *grieve* their collapsing securities.

In another church, a session on nuclear freeze was held. As they sought to convince one another of the rightness of their positions, people chose sides. A sensitive teacher realized that many of the participants were dealing with safety, a temple-of-meaning issue (meaning-perspective). The tone of the class shifted as she helped them *consider* their feelings of insecurity. To their surprise, participants learned that they shared a common fear, even if they could not share common conclusions. The differences did not disappear, but the tone of their conversation was altered as they connected in their mutuality.

Considering, grieving, and *affirming* take time. Much of our teaching begins with startling experiences which call us into decision: family crises, personal illness, national disaster, even a move to a new community. Anything that shakes the foundations of our temples calls us to *consider* meaning and is an opportunity to begin the teaching process. Madeleine L'Engle tells of her response to a day spent in an emergency room, seeing people's lives shattered by accidents. As she *considered* their pain, she *remembered* the resources to which she turned for meaning:

> We turn to stories and pictures and music [exploring] because they show us who and what and why we are, and what our relationship is to life and death, what is essential. . . . [This art] takes the chaos in which we live and shows us structure and pattern, not the structure and pattern of conformity which imprisons but the structure which liberates, sets us free [discerning] to become growing, mature human beings.[14]

Life experience can call us to explore our stories, and those of our traditions, *and* seek to name and decide. Grace empowers our learning.

Beginning with Discerning

Teaching can begin also with corporate or personal decisions.[15] One pastor tells how a congregation's recognition of its changing neighborhood was an opportunity for teaching about the nature of the church. When church members *decided* to remain in the neighborhood, it was necessary to *consider* how to live out that decision. The church's planning process was educational, as people learned even more about themselves and about the gospel. *Attending to* and *exploring* stories of the Hebrew people struggling through the wilderness, and of the early Christian communities, became important resources for them.

Adrienne's vocational choice (chapter 1) was a personal decision. She was a successful teacher who also felt called into full-time church service. She talked with friends and a mentor about the decision, *exploring* resources from the Christian faith and her past experience. She knew that all Christians are called into ministry. God calls people to many careers. Yet, when she *named* her particular call, she was at a new place to learn.

She said, "I'm not in a big hurry to start seminary, and I am. It's a real weird pull, but seminary's not exactly where I am now. What I'm trying to do is lay some groundwork, so that when the time is right, I'll be ready." Her *decision* was clear. She knew she needed to "lay some groundwork." When we have discerned a call or made a decision, we then lay the groundwork by facing two important questions: (1) How do I feel about the decision I have made; can I live with it? (*considering*); and (2) What do I need to study to fulfill that decision? (*exploring*). After laying the groundwork, Adrienne decided not to attend seminary, but to remain in teaching. She searched for a college in which she could express her call to ministry through teaching.

As another example, one congregation *decided* that it was called to address the issue of hunger. Rather than turning to printed curriculum, the members immersed themselves in a study of various agencies that were responding to hunger. They *explored* purpose statements and *considered* alternatives. Then they turned to their theological tradition and struggled to *discern* a plan of action. The tradition challenged experience, and experience challenged tradition. The planning process was a teaching and learning moment: They *considered* their feelings, they *explored* their tradition, and they *named* their actions.

Recall a teaching plan you have used recently. How would it be changed if you began at each of these three starting points: exploring, considering, discerning?

The process of teaching and learning is dynamic: Discerning, exploring, and considering move back and forth. Teachers engage life by calling people to critical reflection and wholeness. Teachers seek to create safe and hospitable spaces, in which people honor and explore as interpreters together. Teachers call us toward wholeness as we share authentically, experience the grace of God, and reach out into the world.

CHAPTER EIGHT

TOWARD WHOLENESS WITH JUSTICE

Leading

Religious education leaders are immersed in life within institutions. We care for those with whom we work, as well as the unnamed ones who are touched by our actions. We strive to live by our meanings, but these intersect and sometimes conflict with those of our congregations, institutions, and communities. We agree upon assignments, set goals, solve problems, and execute decisions. But in these tasks, how do we respond to God and our neighbor? How do we work for justice? How do our concerns for human wholeness engage the transformation of society?

Tasks of Leadership

Helen and Ardis (chapter 6) became leaders in religious education. As they sought to prepare a school curriculum on physical and sexual abuse, they probed the resources of their church, Faith Community Church, a growing congregation in a historic peace denomination. The church both supported them and learned from their actions. Their efforts are a lens through which to examine religious education leadership.

They approached the chair of the Christian Education

committee, requesting support to develop and test in the
church a six-week series on abuse, aimed at elementary
children and their parents. The chair was excited; she
called a special committee meeting. Reaction was mixed.
Some members were afraid that controversy would stunt
the church's growth. Others were reminded of the
church's past leadership on community issues. Amidst the
ambiguity, they formed a task force to study the request.

At the next meeting, they continued to explore: What
would happen if child abuse were uncovered among
church members? Was it right to "interfere" with a school
issue? What were the boundaries of family privacy? How
could they both care and seek justice? Unable to decide,
the committee sought congregational input.

That input was intense and diverse. Some feared
controversy. Others reminded the church of risks it had
taken by speaking out on peace issues and referred to the
denomination's stand on justice. Still others, mostly new
members, reported that they were confused about the
denomination's way of dealing with theological or social
issues. And powerfully, two members risked sharing
personal experience with abuse.

When the CE committee convened again, amidst their
uneasiness, members considered faith commitments,
explored options, and ultimately decided to offer the
class. Old patterns (meaning-perspectives) of understanding the boundary between public and private were
inadequate to address justice for abused children, the
most vulnerable persons in our society. Moreover, the
conviction that faith carries the necessity for public action
was reinforced. Several factors influenced the decision.
First, the two stories of abuse opened them to the need.
Second, Helen was trusted. She had done much for the
church. Third, the pastor provided a rationale: "The
church can deal with issues as painful as this with a sense of

care and love not always possible elsewhere." Fourth, the chairperson's openness to the diversity of positions helped people feel included. Finally, Faith Church's history of integrating faith with life issues was crucial for the decision.

The study went well. As the class unfolded, the teachers realized that the topic was inseparable from issues of self-esteem and the intrinsic worth of each created person. They called for critical reflection about values portrayed by the media. Teaching in the church enabled Helen and Ardis to deal holistically with the dimensions of this crucial issue. Biblical and theological reflection interacted with public concerns. The church enriched the community. In turn, the church's vision of its ministry with children was expanded.

Five dynamics of religious education leadership are evidenced in this case. *First, religious education leaders are called out from the people.* Leaders are not born—they emerge, are nurtured, grow, and develop. In the process of discovering and creating meanings, people *become* leaders. Leaders are not an exclusive group of people. All persons are born with gifts and graces. Many have the interest or hear the call to acquire the understandings and skills necessary to become leaders. Just as Helen, Ardis, the chair of the committee, the members who listened to the congregation, the two who shared their stories, and the pastor—all *became* co-leaders—so we too can develop knowledge and skills to discern and interpret. Circumstances call people into leadership.

Second, leaders interact with their contexts. Educational environments are "open systems." Experiences and concerns of neighborhoods, the larger community, and the world intersect with religious education. Concurrently, religious educators have an opportunity to influence that neighborhood, community, or world.[1] Faith Church, for example, found itself at the center of a community issue because of the public leadership of Helen and Ardis. Once raised, the issue touched deeply the life of the congregation. Two people shared from their pasts. The compromises the church had made for growth were revealed. The tradition of the denomination and the church's leadership on peace issues were remembered.

Open systems are also multilayered. Like a cake, the religious education environment is layered with past traditions, as well as those of current interpreters. Meaning-making occurs in this web of human interactions filled with competing values and self-interests. At Faith Church, the people's experiences, the community's values, the congregation's history of care for the community, and its Christian perspectives interacted to influence a curriculum for education about abuse. We are both shapers and products of our environment.[2] We set directions, plan strategies, and take actions which impact our communities, but our context also impacts our meanings.

Third, we relate to persons and structures in mutuality. Leaders are not mavericks who, without consultation, independently work on their agenda as if it were the group's agenda. At times, we teach. On occasion, we lead. And at still other times, we follow. We influence and are influenced by others.[3] Four of the factors that led to the committee's decision were based on personal relationships: Those who shared their own stories; Helen's care for the congregation; the pastor's support; and the chairperson's inclusion of the views of the congregation.

Mutuality guides the actions of religious education leaders. Mutuality seeks to treat all as equals. Leaders acknowledge the need to provide hospitable spaces in which individuals' meanings can be expressed and honored. When concerns were voiced about how to respond if cases of abuse were identified in the church, the group gave attention. The perspectives of others in the congregation were included in the decision-making. Loving community is grounded in our freedom to make, communicate, and negotiate meanings among one another. Honoring the mutuality of meanings both encourages persons to engage the group's values, and equips them to challenge boundaries and ideas that the rendering of the years has made unintelligible. Holding our meanings in relationship makes it possible for us to "agree to disagree."

What groups or voices influence decisions in your community or church? What groups or voices are ignored?

While community itself is a set of mutual relations, Christian faith affirms that the whole of creation is held together intimately in a mutuality with God.[4] Acknowledging God's presence in history encourages the risk of faith, even when the ground has shifted and our temples of meaning are shaky. The faith tradition teaches us that we are created as children of God, and we are called to participate in the reign and realm of God. Helen and Ardis were convinced that the church's resources were essential for addressing child abuse. Those resources seek to link us with ultimate concerns. In the past, they had led Faith Church to acts of justice. Christian tradition affirms that God is with us, willing just relationships with one another and with creation.

The fourth mark of leadership is vision. Helen, in particular, was clear that God's call to love and justice was directed toward "the least of these." For her, vision was adequate only when it supported and protected the freedom and humanity of the powerless. Her vision empowered her actions.

A purpose, a vision, exists in any relationship of two or more persons. It may be explicit or implicit. Vision sets a course of action. Visionary leadership is contagious.[5] Persons are inspired with purposes relevant to both their histories and their dreams. Leaders fuse the meanings that individuals bring from their life experiences with the purposes and tasks of the group. For example, a person who loves the Gospel of John becomes a good leader for a Lenten study of the passion narrative in John. In linking meaning and life experience, we are empowered with hope to engage new possibilities.

Our visions of the future are rooted in the past. Yet, the past is always remembered in light of present circumstances. Through the use of scripture and tradition, we examine past meanings that informed and guided the actions of our forebears in the faith. Empowered by their witness, we survey the path ahead, exploring options to discern faithful responses to God's call. Each generation has interpreted and appropriated the Christian heritage for its place and time in history, thus providing for its continuity and change.[6]

Visions call us forward into risk and action. Visions empower leaders and communities to remember, reconstruct, and transform meanings. We remember. Many of our tasks and responsibilities are routine, although prior meanings facilitate current actions. Yet, when we face obstacles and challenges, we have to remind ourselves of our commitments. For Helen and Ardis, the church could respond in meaningful ways to child abuse because the church had responded in the past. In its planning, the CE committee needed to remember the risks Faith Church had taken.

Interpretations are always dynamic. New life experiences may render old patterns of meaning unserviceable. Remembering past actions or visions does not always answer a current need. Visions need to be renewed and meanings reconstructed.[7] Although the church had previously addressed public issues in the community, abuse seemed a personal issue for some, inappropriate for the church. As people shared their concerns and together enlarged their previous positions, the class was affirmed.

Finally, the visionary character of leadership occasionally calls for a transformation of meanings. Sometimes a group must change its vision to respond to a changing environment. Transformation may have occurred for some people within Helen's congregation and within the community, but remembering and reconstructing might better describe that congregation's actions.

However, another church, Saint Mark's, illustrates visionary leadership which transforms. Saint Mark's had been the pinnacle of the community. As the neighborhood around it changed and new families of different ethnic heritages moved in, congregants ignored the changes. Members became fewer and lived farther from the church. The neighborhood looked elsewhere for leadership.

The congregants learned that their old meaning-perspective was inadequate for the new context. The transition was painful, but now the members have reached out to the neighborhood's three ethnic groups (Anglo-, Japanese-, and Indian-American). Saint Mark's is becoming a center where people search together for a neighborhood vision. The Christian faith they shared encouraged them to risk.

The older members of the congregation experienced a crumbling of their temples of meaning. Their original vision was not sufficient to account for the new experience. A new vision had to be found. Vision can enable us to transcend boundaries and overturn the soil of eroding foundations, building new structures of meaning.

Leaders learn and live in community. We seek to remember, reconstruct, and transform meanings. Fundamental to all our actions is the responsibility to transform the meaninglessness of persons and groups by constructing experience into coherent and viable meanings. Helen heard the call of the little ones. Her request opened the church and the community to each other. Meaning and mutuality were engendered. Vision, therefore, has both pastoral and prophetic dimensions. We are compassionately concerned for all people, and we join God in actions for justice. Both dimensions are united in our vocations as learners, leaders, and teachers. Vision combines God's action and human action to build individual and collective wholeness.

Fifth, methods for leading are like those for teaching. Deciding is implicitly educational. The three elements of the teaching model (chapter 7) come to play in a community's decisions. The leader is, in fact, a teacher, calling people to *explore* experiences and faith traditions, to *consider* the meanings that guide their lives, and to *discern* the commitments and actions they will take into the world. Leadership usually begins with discernment.

For Helen and Ardis, the development of the school curriculum was a moment of deciding *and* learning. While it would be scrutinized by community leaders before being put into practice, and while it could not contain explicit religious content, Helen and Ardis knew that their theological convictions needed to be tapped as they wrote it, *and* their colleagues in the church consulted. They explored faith commitments; they considered their convictions to see what to affirm and what to relinquish;

and they decided that the content and form of the curriculum should reflect the needs and commitments of the community.

Helen's request also brought the church to a moment of decision and learning. That decision was a moment to discern Faith Church's commitments and actions. The congregation learned much about its own character (the compromises it had made for membership growth and the values of public responsibility that it held deeply). The church was empowered to reclaim values that united faith and life. Many learned why the denomination had been so committed to public action.

Moments of decision in a community are moments for learning. Critical reflection is engendered. The resources of the faith tradition are consulted. Meaning-perspectives are exposed, and people see the compromises they have made, as well as the forces and visions that guide them. Religious leaders know that decisions are not simple; decisions call on all the resources at hand, as well as the meanings that have guided people. Decisions connect meaning and vocation.

The Aim of Leadership

Just as the goal of learning is wholeness with justice (chapter 4), the goal of leadership is wholeness with justice. Educators, pastors, and teachers lead and teach when they seek to create environments that are hospitable and just. Committee chairs teach and lead when they seek to affect a committee's process, so that people explore and consider their meanings in order to discern faithful actions. Church members teach and lead as they call congregations to seek faithfulness. Three concepts—meaningful, critical, and liberating—fill out the meaning of wholeness.[8]

Educational experiences are *meaningful* when they

engage people's life experiences. For example, Saint Mark's, the congregation in the transitional neighborhood, had acted for a time as if the new neighbors were invisible. However, as the members opened themselves to the neighborhood, they also discovered commitments that could be affirmed and others that needed to be grieved. They learned to honor difference. They grieved their isolation. At times, the three ethnic groups celebrated and learned together. At times, they trod on one another's values. Yet, they grew together in their differences. Their actions meaningfully addressed their experiences.

Wholeness is also *critical* and dynamic. We teach in ways that uncover and examine controlling assumptions. Meanings are always shaped within a context. The unequal distribution of social, economic, and political power defines the background within which decisions are made. Power excludes and controls people. Learners need to reflect critically on how their identity has been shaped. For example, the marginalization of persons based on race, class, gender, or age has led to the silencing of their voices and the ignoring of their experiences. Religious education that moves toward wholeness challenges the grip of power. It recognizes the dreams, upholds the histories, and acknowledges visions of those who have been silenced.

Finally, wholeness *liberates*. We listen to ourselves, to others, to the world, and to God as we build our communities. Individuals and groups are freed of the need to conform to be accepted. Education is never neutral or value-free. It has political consequences. Those with power try to control its aims and processes. However, education, rooted in the Exodus and the acts of Jesus, equips us with vision and motivates our efforts toward more just relations. Religious educators and learners must negotiate their interpretations and actions amid a complex of ideologies, values, and self-interests which often conflict. We need to affirm our differences and build coalitions of care and justice.

Where do you see "wholeness that liberates" in the Bible? Where does it happen in your life?

A commitment to meaningful, critical, and liberating reflection often means exposing values that control and limit people. One church, for example, addressed our culture's obsession when it revised a long-standing program. The educator challenged the men's group's "Breakfast with Santa" for children. She believed the children were mixing "I want" (Santa's gifts) with "God gives" (grace and justice). Her challenge was met with heated arguments. Making the decision involved negotiation about the meaning of Christmas. Conflicting values were addressed. The breakfast was revised. Today the church holds a "Breakfast in Bethlehem" to honor their Christian witness.

We need to learn to resist restrictive practices of society. Leaders work toward personal wholeness, while also moving toward more equitable and just relations among others. Only when both individual and collective wholeness are the aim of leadership are human needs addressed, visions connected with ultimate concerns, and communities nurtured and empowered in the search for meaning and truth.

Connecting Meaning and Vocation

Leaders agree upon assignments, set ministry goals, solve problems, work for justice, and execute decisions in light of their meanings. Their decisions affect their communities. Leaders plan, set structures, and establish processes for learning—that is, work to establish hospitable and just spaces where interpreters learn together by practicing the presence of God. But how do leaders know what to do? How do they respond to the neighbor and to God? How do leaders challenge persons and their communities to wholeness and justice?

Leaders explore, consider, and discern. They also influence communities to explore, consider, and discern. The method of teaching we identified in chapter 7 is also a way to define how we will live out our vocation in the world.[9] As leaders plan to act, they ask questions about: (1) themselves; (2) the people with whom they work; (3) the environments in which they work; (4) God's call.

PREPARING FOR LEADERSHIP DECISIONS

I. *Describe* the situation, issue, or decision to be addressed.
II. *Reflect* on the following questions:
  1. What commitments, experiences, and vision do I (the leader) bring to this situation?
  2. What are the values, experiences, and visions of the people with whom I work? How do their commitments interact with the situation?
  3. What is the context within which I work? What commitments, limitations, openings for ministry are present in the context?
  4. What is God's call to us in this situation? Seek to discern this with the community.
III. *Develop* a process to engage the community in exploring, considering, and discerning.

1. *What commitments, experiences, and vision do I (the leader) bring to this situation?* Just as teachers have convictions that influence classes, leaders are empowered by their own experiences and convictions. They also have practices with which they are comfortable. Helen's convictions about abuse affected both the curriculum she was writing and the way she influenced the church. She believed that abuse violated a fundamental faith conviction: The sanctity of a person. Abuse, therefore, was an issue of both faith and justice. Confronting it could not be avoided by the church.

Management consultant Donald Schoen has used the image "reflective practitioner" to describe professionals.[10] That image can be extended to all leaders of education. The leader is a *practitioner*—involved in actions that are significant for others. Therefore, a leader's actions need to be responsible, interactive, and engaged. Moreover, the leader is *reflective*. Leading is not simply the application of a particular skill to a particular situation—neither magical nor routine. Rather, leadership is informed practice. Schoen talks about the leader as artist, involved in a creative process using the resources at hand.

Christian educator Maria Harris offers a complementary image: The teacher/leader is an artist who, with others, "forms" the community.[11] The process of reflection which empowers teaching (chapter 7) is the same process that empowers a leader. For example, *exploring* includes gathering information, attending to resources (social, theological, political), and remembering one's past experiences.

Another metaphor for reflective practice is "practical theologian." As one who invests energy in others' lives, a religious leader stands in the midst of a dynamic tradition—looking back toward the witnesses of the faith who sought to discern God's call, looking forward to the vision of the reign and realm of God—and seeking prayerfully and humbly, in community, to discern God's call.[12] The exploring and remembering that shape the commitments of a religious education leader include *personal experience, skills brought to a situation, one's values and meaning-perspectives, and the faith tradition in which one stands.* Helen stood within a dynamic tradition. Her church sought to discern God's call.

Every decision participates in the shaping of a dynamic tradition. The concerns about membership that influenced Paul's correspondence with Christians in Corinth were leadership decisions. Paul could only seek to influence people. Some listened and others opposed, but all were trying to be faithful. Paul's recorded actions have become guides for us. Likewise, the church's controversies through the centuries inform our actions today. In each local situation, we are reshaping that tradition. We ask anew, "How can we be faithful?"

Many educational leaders are responsible for programming. They arrange programs, recruit others, define curriculum, set structures, and evaluate. Each action is an effort to be faithful to their commitments. In other situations, educational leaders are not in charge. Nonetheless, even here, as they participate with others in decisions, their vision informs the meanings and passion they share.

2. *What are the values, experiences, and visions of the people with whom I work?* Leaders bring commitments; so do others who participate in decisions. While all decisions cannot be made in a group, nor need they be, each decision should honor the fact that we are a community of interpreters. As teachers must determine strategies that invite learners into the process, so leaders also influence and carry out tasks that invite the community into the processes of learning and deciding. For example, at Faith Church, the new members, so important to its growth,

were not fully included. The church's future depended upon sharing and struggling together, upon mutuality.

It seems paradoxical. Attention to the uniqueness of each person's experience does not negate the claim that only in relationship is human wholeness ultimately possible. As educator Henry Giroux calls us to recognize, students and teachers "come from different histories and embody different experiences, linguistic practices, cultures, and talents."[13] Honoring individuality means addressing differences. The paradox is that, amidst the difference, people must work together to interpret experience and engage in vocation.

Mutuality does not demand conformity or harmony, yet the distinguishing characteristic of mutuality is participation in decisions that affect our life together.[14] Many in Helen's church supported her efforts because their concerns were being heard, and because they recognized an important project. Mutuality means taking into account the commitments that participants bring to decisions. The theology and vocation of a community are shaped in mutual interaction. Actions today set traditions for the future.

3. *What is the context within which I work?* Context includes both the environment within a group and the wider community. Leaders at Faith Church needed to attend to both the environment *within* the congregation (the CE committee, the classroom, the church) and to the meanings and commitments brought into the congregation from the *wider* environment (the community).

First, even the use of space affects the character of the educational environment. Management consultant Edgar Schein argues that "placement of oneself in relation to others symbolizes social distance and membership."[15] Educational leaders make choices about the physical objects present in rooms, based on whether they will enhance or inhibit learning, teaching, and decision-making. For example, a children's classroom should invite children. Furniture needs to be scaled appropriately. Provision needs to be made for children to read the scriptures, worship, and work to make meanings. The very presence of a worship center encourages children and teachers to make connections between education and worship. The religious education leader evaluates the use of space.

Educational environments carry social meaning. The distance between the chairs and their arrangement in the room communicate nonverbally. Different uses of space generate different feelings between leaders, learners, and teachers.[16] If physical distance between leader and co-learners is too close, persons may feel an intrusion. If the distance is too far, persons may feel unwanted or excluded. The use of space increases or decreases our trust, encouragement, and sense of belonging. A circle of chairs is most conducive to sharing feelings mutually. A lectern faced by rows of chairs creates authority for a speaker and diminishes the individuality of participants. The way we use space is no routine matter.

Many other aspects of the physical environment carry meanings as well. Wall color, the clothes we wear, lighting levels, and sound quality are some of the physical components which leaders can manipulate. How do the items in the room limit our thinking? For instance, art work that pictures the disciples as blond and blue-eyed is not only inaccurate but marginalizes other racial groups. Depicting Jesus as passive limits our understanding of his power and righteous anger.

Second, context reaches out into the wider world. Our work within a church is connectional—connected to the communities and lives and neighborhoods and issues of the wider world. A local church is influenced by the contexts that shape its members. Decisions made about a community, such as the widening of a road, or zoning, affect the church within that community.

Our responsibilities are always grounded in particular times and places. Actions that we take in a church will also affect others. When we believe that our meanings are important, we find ways of communicating these to the public.

In describing the contemporary world, educators Stanley Aronowitz and Henry Giroux emphasize interconnections. Our world no longer consists of isolated nations and communities. In an "age of instant information, global networking . . . the historically and socially constructed nature of meaning becomes evident, dissolving universalizing claims to history, truth, or class."[17] As religious leaders, we work within particular cultures. Learners and teachers need to be invited to examine their assumptions and values, as well as explore the limits of meaning-perspectives and action strategies. More than at any other time in history, we are aware that the silencing of marginalized voices leads to self-deception. Interpreting together demands critical reflection upon the meanings we use to construct the stories of our lives.

Name some images you have of your future. Examine (critical reflection) the assumptions and commitments that make them important.

4. *What is God's call to us in this situation?* As religious
education leaders, at the center of our lives is *practicing the
presence of God.* What can we do to open ourselves to God's
presence and activity in our midst? Theological educator
Craig Dykstra reminds us that the church provides
practices to assist us in discerning God's call.[18] Practices are
dynamic. We need to think of *practicing,* of always seeking
more adequate ways to be open to God. John Wesley
described these practices as means of grace, by which
persons conformed their lives to God: prayer, Bible
reading, acts of charity, and the sacraments. As we decide,
we seek to discern God's call.

The heroes, heroines, and prophets of our Christian
heritage reconstructed and transformed their experiences into images of what could be. They looked forward
to justice where injustice occurred. They dreamed of a
better world. Locating our identity in this tradition calls us
to be open to the new thing that God is doing in our
midst—that is, transforming us and our world toward
justice and wholeness.

We can trust and risk entering deeply into the pain of a
context because we know that God is with us. Saint Mark's
Church had to make a decision in its changing neighborhood. It could insulate itself, or it could reach out to new
neighbors. Empowered by the vision of God's wide,
outreaching arms, the church risked. The opening of its
doors to shared fellowship also encouraged people in the
neighborhood to risk.

Prayer is at the heart of our decisions. Through grace,
we know that God empowers us with hope and possibilities. We live now in the day of justice and equality, and
yet—not yet. Our decisions are acts of discernment in
which we seek to join with God in working toward the new
creation.

Leadership as Discernment

Exploring:

Gather information

Assess commitments

For the purpose of living holistically and justly into the world

Discerning

Considering

Weigh options

Envisioning the Future

Leadership connects meanings and vocation. People listen critically to their meanings, probe the Christian traditions, engage their contexts, and participate in the ongoing shaping and reshaping of Christian faith and practice, in light of God's care and call. As Christians, we are plural: male and female, young and older, and culturally diverse, formed differently by history and geography. We learn, teach, and lead, in an effort to bring God's vision of wholeness and justice to fruition. Vision inspires leadership. Practicing presence provides guidance. Procedures honor the mutuality of interpreters learning together. And structures need to be hospitable and just.

Working in institutions and living in communities—
these situations, in themselves, are educational. Such
education can either empower us or block and inhibit our
options. We learn how to make meaning. We engage in
tasks that remind us of what is central. Religions teach
through their explicit telling and retelling of stories and
creeds (beliefs) (chapter 3). Religions also teach by
influencing people's behavior. *Codes* of living are taught
and expected of others. For example, many Asian
religions teach the value of the elders. In Buddhism, *bun
kuhn* is the practice through which elders are respected
and protected. Society is based on a reciprocity of
care—parents for the young and the child for aging
parents.

Religions teach through worship and ritual practices
(*cultus*). A funeral reminds people that life, no matter how
frail, is lived in relation to God. Rituals like baptism,
confirmation, and marriage, conducted within the community of faith, connect daily living to the Holy. Religion
is also taught through *community,* as people interact by
practicing beliefs, standards, and rituals. Religious education leaders are sensitive to the way communities teach,
as well as to the teaching that occurs within classrooms.

For example, Shirley, a church educator, worked with
her congregation to create a "Celebration of Ministries."
The celebration was held on the day of the congregational
meeting, when goals and programs for the past year were
reviewed and plans set for the future. The planning
committee wanted to encourage the understanding that
all baptized Christians are ministers. As the celebration
was planned, Shirley consulted with each task force and
mission group within the congregation. She created a
script that highlighted the stated mission goals of the
congregation and the involvement of individuals in
mission. Using the script, the planning committee

designed a worship service that affirmed all those ministries.

The process itself was educational, as members of task groups explored their commitments, understood their relationship to other ministries of the congregation, grieved as they named their failures, and began to redefine their vocations. The worship service and the congregational meeting were settings for learning as people shared their lives and made meaning together.

Another example of community religious education occurs within a neighborhood of Hiroshima, Japan. Yoshihiro works as a Christian community organizer with several congregations, in efforts for peace and justice. Within Hiroshima is the Peace Park which reminds the world of the atomic explosion in 1945. Yoshihiro argues that the park itself is caught in the causes of war. A memorial to twenty thousand Korean prisoners who died in the explosion had to be built outside the park fence. Enlarging the park's boundaries to include the memorial is an educational and justice activity chosen by the community organization.

In a protest to the mayor, Yoshihiro proclaimed, "Peace cannot be a reality until the monument is inside the park. War is rooted in injustice and racism. The exclusion of the Korean monument is an example of injustice."

As an education leader, Yoshihiro is helping the people of the community reflect on meanings embodied within its practices. Much of his time is spent in an "outcast" community, working with church and community leaders to seek aid and justice for the poor, and to provide education through a day-care and community-education center. He also spends time with congregations that teach peace education in their nursery schools and church schools, in order to join parents, children, and community in peacemaking.

Meaning is made in community. The work of church educators to affect the environment of the church, and the activity of community educators to affect neighborhoods and towns, are educational processes. People become aware of their commitments as they engage in processes of reflection and meaning-making. Whether we are planning the structure for next year's Sunday school program, designing a celebration of ministries in the congregation, or creating structures to promote peace, we act on our meanings. May our vocations be infused with God's call. God lures us forward "to do justice, and to love kindness, and to walk humbly" (Micah 6:8).

POSTLUDE

———

Many days and years of our lives pass smoothly in a comfortable blur. We do not question the meanings upon which we depend. The temples of meaning which we have built stand sturdily, needing little repair and demanding little notice. We hold meaninglessness at bay—out of our consciousness. Yet occasionally, meaninglessness overwhelms us, threatening our temples, causing us to worry about their foundations and the strength of their weight-bearing structures.

Such a time occurred when Jane, a youth minister, talked with several teenagers in the church hallway about Bryan's absence.

"Bryan's in the hospital," she said. "He checked into the drug rehabilitation unit." Shock enveloped the group.

"He was here for youth group last Sunday."

"He's in my history class."

"I didn't know."

Jane listened. The young people asked what they could do to help.

"Let's go to see him and let him know we love him. He needs us right now," said Jane.

They were frightened. Bryan had seemed so like them, a good kid who tried hard—part of their group. He did not seem any more discouraged or fragile than they. They wondered whether they could withstand the pressures of *their* lives. Their meanings were challenged.

A young woman gave birth to a son. Barbara took care of herself during the pregnancy, eating healthy foods,

181

seeing a doctor regularly, and waiting expectantly for the new life. Minutes after the birth, a team of doctors entered her room to tell her that her baby had Down's Syndrome. Barbara was in shock. The dreams she had for him had to be revised. His possibilities were more limited. Suddenly, her life seemed so complicated.

Later, when her pastor visited, Barbara told of asking God over and over in the solitude of the early morning, "Why? How do you think I can handle this? You know how selfish I am. Why would you send me this little child who is going to need so much care?"

"And what are you feeling now?" the pastor asked.

"I don't know. I just don't know. But I know John and I are going to love him. He is our little boy."

"Those 'why' questions are hard. You may have to keep asking for a long time. You may never have an answer. . . . He's a child of God. We're *all* going to love him, and we love you," said the pastor with an understanding smile and a lump in her throat.

"Maybe you're asking the wrong question," she continued. "Maybe we should be asking what resources God is offering us to help us understand. Maybe we should be asking what new possibilities God offers in the midst of this challenge."

Meanings were threatened. Just when we think we are in control and life is predictable, something unexpected intervenes; we must reconsider our temples of meaning.

The young people at Bethel, the church in the inner city, were almost shattered by John's death. At twelve, he had been a member of one of the neighborhood gangs, but he had left the gang, joined their after-school program, and become an honors student in high school. John was seventeen, was to graduate in a month, and had high hopes. As he left a party, a car drove by. A youth who shouted slogans of the rival neighborhood gang shot him in the chest.

"Is it worth it?" one of the others pleaded.

"I hope we make a difference," sighed a volunteer. Even with their convictions and the support of the community, many people at Bethel Church faced the meaninglessness of a senseless death. Like many who live in a violent and racist society, they had to question the effectiveness of their efforts at transformation. As a nation, we faced meaninglessness when Martin Luther King, Jr., and Bobby Kennedy were killed by assassins' bullets. Meaninglessness shatters hope. We plead for understanding.

These intersections where persons bring their histories and their meanings for questioning and reconstruction are moments for religious education. Religious education is not confined to a classroom, but can occur anywhere hospitable and just space is created, where people can practice God's presence and interpret together the meanings of experiences, where even questions as profound and difficult as these are welcomed into the conversation.

Worship often becomes an intersection where meaning-making takes place. When Dr. Svendson, the beloved pastor of a large church, lost his father, he led worship on Sunday as always. People who knew of his loss marveled at his control.

However, near the end of the hour, he paused to say, "I want to change our final hymn. Many of you know that my father passed away last night. He was ninety years old. He lived a full life. He has been very important to me. I will miss him. But I celebrate his rich life and his passing on into the church eternal. I want you to celebrate with me.

Will you sing with me one of his favorite hymns, 'Children
of the Heavenly Father'?"

The congregation sang, many straining through tears.
They empathized with their pastor, feeling his loss. They
also thanked God for the meaningful life that had just
ended. They shared in the grief and the joy together,
reinforcing their temples of meaning. Meaninglessness
seemed overwhelming, but in community, it receded.

A community project provided Lee-Suk an opportunity
for religious education. She was a bright child who
excelled. She did not know her parents, one of whom had
been American, the other Korean. Despite her accom-
plishments, others made fun of her because of her
ancestry. Yet at college, she discovered love and acceptance in a prayer group. She began to tutor in a college
ministry at a Korean night school, working with the
poorest (the *minjung*) to help them claim their rights and
power. As she reflected on their lives and her own, a new
self unfolded, one that was more whole and just. The
revelation of her own fragility helped her to accept God's
claim on her life. Her story is parabolic, calling for justice
and connection in a world of separation. The meanings
she found empower her to work for human rights.

Meaning and Meaninglessness

Meaning and meaninglessness, order and chaos, are
always in tension. At moments of meaning and order, life
makes sense. At moments of meaninglessness and chaos,
life is upturned. We live precariously balanced between
meanings that remain and renew, and structures that
deteriorate and threaten. At times, such as when an
earthquake strikes, our understanding of a created world

order is besieged by chaos. Sometimes we experience loneliness; sometimes, solitude. Sometimes we experience alienation; sometimes, community. The dialectic persists. Meaning is fragile. We never are quite sure which is more powerful: meaning, or its loss.

For example, competing ideologies and hatreds appear to make peace and community impossible. Yet, Japanese children place handmade paper cranes for peace at the Hiroshima monument, a reminder of the atomic explosion. Their simple act speaks of a connectedness which transcends political differences. Their act also teaches us that one small gesture can bring meaning and hope.

A mid-life crisis may signal the power of meaninglessness. Changes in our lives, such as children leaving home, can precipitate a reevaluation of roles. Often, a woman who has devoted herself to nurturing will wonder about the value of her life with no one to care for. Others may burst forth at mid-life with generativity; creative projects or new careers are begun.

Individuals are compelled by the experiences of their lives to ask questions about meaning. We often do not have a language to articulate these questions, nor enough distance to see them in a larger context. However, the community of faith provides both language and support. Religious education is conversation about our lives, in light of God's presence. We read through our temporal experiences to the eternal. Meaning-making connects us with ourselves, others, the creation, and God. The search for meaning calls us toward wholeness and justice.

Religious Education as Incarnation

The religious educator creates spaces where meaning-making conversations can occur in light of God's presence. The church hallway, a telephone conversation, a hospital room, a picket line, the sanctuary, a community council, a visit to Central America, a church task force, or a meeting over a cup of coffee—any of these could be such a place. We discern, we explore, and we consider. In the midst of important meaning-making conversations, the religious educator's goal is to embody God's will for wholeness and vocation for all people. Thus, religious education is *incarnational*.

Jesus is *the* Incarnation. Jesus lived uniquely, led by the light of God. God was present in his healings, relationships, teachings, and love. As Jesus touched others, sometimes they too incarnated God's love. God continues to call us into wholeness—our full humanity. Incarnational religious education embodies God's love and purpose, so that we may reach out to others in transformative relationships. In other words, we are incarnations with a lower-case "i." In our love, our acts of healing, our work for justice, our claiming of our identities, and the fulfilling of our vocations, we make God's presence concrete.

A primary *method* that enables incarnation is mutual conversation. Christian religious education has been bound up in schooling structures. Knowing information is not sufficient. Meaning requires a place where people can talk together about the important things God is doing in their lives.

"The church school of the future will be less like a school and more a *home*," claimed Bishop John Vincent in 1905, at the end of his career as a founder of Sunday schools. "Its keynote will not be *recitation* but *conversation* . . . natural, simple, wisely conducted conversations with a view to the promotion of practical and spiritual life."[1] As Bishop Vincent reminded us, the structures of conversation are simpler, but require greater depth and authenticity.

The word *conversation* may seem ordinary, even

flippant. Certainly we do waste much time in empty
conversations, hiding ourselves and pretending. The
religious education conversation also is ordinary, about
events of life. But in it, the depth of each of us is plumbed
and connected with the depth of God. We learn to live in
light of eternity.

Critical reflection on living becomes the curriculum for
religious education. We examine the meanings our lives
embody, so that we may more fully incarnate wholeness
and justice. Therefore, we do not teach concepts, creeds,
or images alone. Learners do not merely recite content.
Instead, teaching occurs in the midst of life, embracing us
as whole persons, as well as the tradition. Death and birth,
loneliness and relatedness, meaning and meaninglessness
become subjects—the content of the religious education
curriculum. Issues of loss, of limits, of gift, and of justice
call us to reflect and act.

Conversations about our actions, the incarnations of
our meanings, involve risk. Participants must feel safe
enough to share their commitments with others. We must
be willing to risk telling another of our strength and pain
and listen to that person's strength and pain. Risking
opens up meaning questions. We may need to change.

Barbara risked when she told her pastor that she could
not understand why God had sent her the baby. She risked
by sharing her feelings of inadequacy and selfishness. And
the pastor, who wondered if Barbara might be asking the
wrong questions, risked sharing her own meanings as well.
The pastor also faced a crisis of meaning and needed
resources to deal with her own grief. The two women
opened themselves to new understandings in mutual
conversation.

The *context* for the conversation is our embeddedness in
history, including the people who touch our lives as well as
the ever-widening network of systems that have formed

us. We deal with injustice and the powers that limit
people's freedom to make meaning and secure a future.
Each of us brings to the intersection our own meaning-
perspectives, with their baggage (our cultural blinders,
our limits) and our beliefs (meaning-schemes). But the
wisdom of the tradition, as well as the accumulated
interpretations of our culture, also enrich and challenge
our personal and corporate histories.

Risky, meaning-making conversations characterize incarnational religious education, calling us into connectedness and thereby into justice-seeking relationships in
creation. We endeavor to become whole persons, living
and acting in light of God's love.

The Incarnational Religious Educator

While the *goal* of Christian religious education is to
incarnate wholeness and justice, the process begins as
religious educators seek to create hospitable and just
spaces in which to practice God's presence. We *invite*
others, by our very "being," into the process of meaning-
making. More than being mere role models, we too inhabit
that space; we do not stand above or outside the space.
Meaning-making profoundly focuses us on our own
struggles for meaning, as well as on the construction
projects of others. We are vulnerable. We must be
authentic. Incarnational religious education may require
simpler structures, but it asks more of the educator. We
are fragile together and searching together to embody the
call of God for justice in all creation.

Seeking justice together begins with opening ourselves to
the voices of others. In some mysterious way, even though
all of us are threatened by meaninglessness, we can
support—stand beside—persons as they make meaning,
discovering who they are and what they will do. Our

vocation is to work to create structures which empower people to speak and listen, to risk in safety, and to live wholly and interconnectedly. Lee-Suk risked herself and her pain as she tutored at the night school. The people she met became a great gift to her as she was born into a new identity of acceptance and service.

Standing beside another is dynamic, not static. We offer energy. Those who receive energy are energized and send it back. Thus, the incarnational religious educator is both a source and a receiver of energy. When we open ourselves to another, we enter into the reality of the other and experience life somewhat as the other does. One who truly listens soon comes to respect and love. We are listeners and lovers.

In addition to these relational qualities, the incarnational educator is *attuned to structural possibilities and teachable moments.* The pastor who spoke with Barbara about the meaning of her baby's life was alert to a teachable moment. The young mothers' group to which Barbara belonged provided a structural possibility for dealing with the questions that arose out of their grief and disappointment. Brought together for their regular meeting, the women shared their feelings. The mothers shook their heads in shock.

"How should we feel?" asked Bonnie. "I feel sad and angry. Is it O.K. to be angry?" They talked of how they felt, and they affirmed their love for this baby and his parents. They reconstructed meanings about parenthood and God's gift of life.

Helping in that meaning-making was the mother of another child with Down's Syndrome. She talked with the group about what it was like to care for her son, Tommy, and how the other mothers could support Barbara. As the women recalled the many gifts they had experienced in knowing Tommy, they expressed their belief that all life is

God's gift. They recalled Tommy's love and enthusiasm. They reconstructed their temples of meaning. Life had created a teachable moment. The religious educator capitalized on a structural possibility with the sharing group which met weekly. All those present—the religious educator, the experienced mother with wisdom, and each member of the group—participated mutually in seeking to make meaning.

Whether in personal crises or in social upheaval, the religious educator incarnates God's love and points toward discerning God's call. Meaning and vocation are claimed as we commit ourselves to justice and wholeness.

An Invitation to Incarnation

The Christian religious educator invites others into incarnation. We envision. We hope. We pray that each of us will discover our vocation to be whole and will work for justice. As educator Paulo Freire declares, we teach so that people "may discover through existential experience that their present way of life is irreconcilable with their vocation to become fully human."[2] We teach for new life. The invitation to incarnation has three movements: (1) to explore at the intersection; (2) to practice theological reflection; and (3) to call into ministry (chapter 6).

When we explore at the intersection, we engage *meaning*. We bring together life and history and community. We work to form a faith we can live by. Travis brought to the intersection a theology which encouraged him to believe that he could excel at sports through faith. He also brought a seminary experience which urged him toward justice and social action. He weighed these points of view and found his convictions leading him to become a conscientious objector, supported by his deep Christian faith. In the intersection, our questioning conversations place our meanings on the scales of God's justice. Travis' faith was transformed in the intersection.

We practice theological reflection in an effort to discern *identity*. We learn who we are in light of God's call, putting the Christian story into an ever-deepening dialogue with our lived experience. To put it another way, we seek to create an intersection where we can draw upon the wisdom of the tradition and our own experience in order to know who we are. The young people of Bethel Church came to know their identity as they painted murals about their neighborhood, their people, and God's actions in history. The paintings contained images of oppressive structures, as well as showing the power of the youth. Experience, examined and explored, yielded identity. Even when confronted with John's death, they discovered that because of their support for one another they could still work for change in the community.

Our actions are empowered by meanings. Identity leads to *vocation* as we engage the call to ministry. Adrienne considered changing her career because of an encounter with God. All of us must consider changing our actions in the quest for wholeness and justice.

Each of us is an educator when we invite others into meaning-making conversations. Our goal is incarnation, both for ourselves and for other participants. We hold our vocations up to scrutiny as we stand beside others who also hold theirs up to scrutiny.

Grace and Hope on the Journey

To embody the love of God and invite others into a community of love and justice—this is the highest ideal. Yet that is the goal of incarnational religious education. In a world where meaninglessness engulfs us, how can we claim such a high ideal?

There is only one answer: Through the amazing grace of God. The scriptures attest again and again that God's grace brings about the impossible. God came into human form as a baby, born to a poor young woman named Mary.

Mary was incredulous: "How can this be?"

And the angel explained, "Nothing will be impossible with God" (Luke 1:34, 37).

In Luke, the "impossibility" that Mary carried became the "possibility" for the world. Mary's song poignantly and powerfully points to the promise of God's reign. Jesus promises food for the hungry, power for the powerless, freedom for captives, meaning for those in despair, and justice for the oppressed (Luke 4). To discover grace is to know that God lures the "impossibilities" of life into possibility.

In Madeleine L'Engle's retelling of the Christian story, grace undergirds life and simultaneously calls us to work, to embody justice fully in living: "Possible things are easy to believe. The Glorious Impossibles are what bring joy to our hearts, hope to our lives, songs to our lips."[3] Indeed, the moments in which we have caught glimpses of God's grace offer hope and courage for the journey. Through relationships of love and justice, we experience the glorious impossibles.

God's grace enlivens hope in our moments of meaning-making (religious education): Moments when we stand beside another who offers mutuality—a relationship built on trust and authenticity; moments when our faith community reaches out in healing love; moments when we break through our cultural blinders to see another more clearly and more justly; moments when we combat oppression; moments when we experience life in light of the eternal. God's grace is there before us. God's grace provides hope as we struggle to make meaning in our lives.

What greater privilege can there be than to stand beside others in that struggle for meaning and vocation? To create, along with other participants in the search for meaning and vocation, a hospitable and just space in which to practice the presence of God—this is the calling of the religious educator. To seek to embody in one's very being the human connectedness which brings wholeness and justice—this is the vision that calls the religious educator forward. Come and join in the dance, for there is joy in this glorious impossible. God invites us to partnership!

NOTES

Introduction

1. *The United Methodist Newscope* (April 10, 1992):3.
2. Jack L. Seymour and Donald Miller, eds., *Contemporary Approaches to Christian Education* (Nashville: Abingdon Press, 1982); Jack Seymour, Robert T. O'Gorman, and Charles R. Foster, *The Church in the Education of the Public: Refocusing the Task of Religious Education* (Nashville: Abingdon Press, 1984).
3. Parker Palmer, *To Know As We Are Known: A Spirituality of Education* (San Francisco: Harper & Row, 1983).
4. Yvonna S. Lincoln and Egon G. Guba, *Naturalistic Inquiry* (Beverly Hills: Sage Publications, 1985).
5. Joseph V. Crockett, *Teaching Scripture from an African-American Perspective* (Nashville: Discipleship Resources, 1990).
6. We realize that some people, because of illness or injury, seem to lose the possibility of meaning. Yet even these people can experience the gift of meaning as we all struggle to understand and address their needs. For the power of meaning, see Oliver Sacks, *The Man Who Mistook His Wife for a Hat* (New York: Harper Perennial, 1990), pp. 29, 111-12.
7. Sallie McFague, "An Earthly Theological Agenda," *The Christian Century* 108 (January 2-9, 1991):14.

Chapter 1: Temples of Meaning

1. All the persons referred to in this chapter are real. We have changed the names to preserve privacy. Some are from the life-history interview data in Margaret Ann Durham [Crain], *An Ethnographic Study of Perspectives on Authority of Adult Sunday School Participants: Hearing the Voices* (Ed. D. dissertation, Vanderbilt University, 1991).
2. James Michener, "Home," *American Way* (Sept. 1, 1991):67.
3. Jack Mezirow, *Transformative Dimensions of Adult Learning* (San Francisco: Jossey-Bass, 1991), p. 10.
4. Robert Coles, *The Spiritual Life of Children* (Boston: Houghton Mifflin Co., 1990), p. xv.
5. Renita J. Weems, *Just a Sister Away* (San Diego: Lura Media, 1988), p. 3.
6. Joseph V. Crockett, *Teaching Scripture from an African-American Perspective* (Nashville: Discipleship Resources, 1990). The four strategies he describes illustrate how images orient people in the worlds of meaning.
7. Dan P. McAdams, *Power, Intimacy, and the Life Story: Personological Inquiries into Identity* (New York: Guilford Press, 1989), p. 18.
8. Sharon Parks, *The Critical Years: The Young Adult Search for a Faith to Live By* (San Francisco: Harper & Row, 1986), p. xv.
9. Madeleine L'Engle, *The Summer of the Great Grandmother* (New York: Seabury Press, 1974), p. 130.

10. Wilfred Cantwell Smith, *Faith and Belief* (Princeton: University Press, 1979), p. 137.
11. McAdams, *Power, Intimacy, and the Life Story*, pp. 25, 18.
12. James W. Fowler, *Becoming Adult, Becoming Christian: Adult Development and Christian Faith* (San Francisco: Harper & Row, 1984), p. 95.
13. Roy G. D'Andrade, "Cultural Meaning Systems," *Culture Theory*, ed. Richard A. Shweder and Robert A. LeVine (Cambridge: University Press, 1984), pp. 96-101.
14. Parks, *The Critical Years*, p. 24.

Chapter 2: Seeing with New Eyes

1. John (Fire) Lame Deer and Richard Erdoes, *Lame Deer: Seeker of Visions* (New York: Washington Square Press, 1972), p. 96.
2. Ibid.
3. Ibid., pp. 96-97.
4. Ibid., p. 97.
5. Jack Mezirow, *Transformative Dimensions of Adult Learning* (San Francisco: Jossey-Bass, 1991), p. 16.
6. Alex Kotlowitz, *There Are No Children Here* (New York: Doubleday, 1991), p. 51.
7. Mezirow, *Transformative Dimensions*, p. 42.
8. Ibid., p. 44.
9. Several books which examine the meaning of faith and its role in human development include James Fowler, *Stages of Faith: The Psychology of Human Development and the Quest for Meaning* (San Francisco: Harper & Row, 1981); H. Richard Niebuhr, *Faith on Earth: An Inquiry into the Structure of Human Faith*, ed. Richard R. Niebuhr (New Haven: Yale University Press, 1989); Sharon Parks, *The Critical Years: The Young Adult Search for a Faith to Live By* (San Francisco: Harper & Row, 1986); and Wilfred Cantwell Smith, *Faith and Belief* (Princeton: University Press, 1979).
10. For a discussion of the central role of language in faith, see Daniel Patte, *Paul's Faith and the Power of the Gospel*, chap. 1 (Philadelphia: Fortress Press, 1983).
11. See Jack L. Seymour, *Praying the Gospel of Mark* (Nashville: The Upper Room, 1988).
12. As quoted in Mezirow, *Transformative Dimensions*, p. 19.

Chapter 3: Amazing Grace

1. For descriptions of the power of work/mission trips, see Tom Montgomery-Fate, *Building Worlds, Challenging Boundaries: Appalachia Service Project* (Johnson City, Tenn.: Appalachia Service Project, 1991); and Alice Frazer Evans, Robert A. Evans, and William Bean Kennedy, *Pedagogies for the Non-Poor*, "Traveling for Transformation" (Maryknoll: Orbis Books, 1987), pp. 162-85.
2. Andrew Greeley, *The Religious Imagination* (Los Angeles: Sadlier, 1981), p. 17.
3. Belden C. Lane, "Dragons of the Ordinary: The Discomfort of Common Grace," *The Christian Century* 108 (August 21-28, 1991):772.

4. Ibid., p. 774. These are his words describing two kinds of grace: The power that miraculously rescues us from loss *and* the sustenance found in daily life.
5. For a discussion of Wesley's theology of grace, see Colin Williams, *John Wesley's Theology Today* (Nashville: Abingdon Press, 1960), chaps. 3, 5, 10.
6. Sharon Parks, *The Critical Years: The Young Adult Search for a Faith to Live By* (San Francisco: Harper & Row, 1986), pp. 24-26.
7. Ibid., p. 26.
8. Rita Nakashima Brock, *Journeys by Heart: A Christology of Erotic Power* (New York: Crossroad, 1991), p. 17. See also Nel Noddings, *Caring: A Feminine Approach to Ethics and Moral Education* (Berkeley: University of California Press, 1984), p. 6. This philosopher of education maintains that our ethics, our vocations, are rooted in our caring connection with others. Joy results when we find others to stand with us in moments of pain, injustice, and brokenness. See also the poignant description of joy as promise in Madeleine L'Engle, *Circle of Quiet* (San Francisco: Harper & Row, 1972), pp. 124-25.
9. For one discussion of the relation of faith to grace in the Christian scriptures, see Rom. 3:21-26; 5:1ff.
10. Catherine L. Albanese, *American Religions and Religion* (Belmont, Cal.: Wadsworth Publishing Co., 1981), pp. 3-5.
11. Ordinary religion is, to use Peter Berger's phrase, making a *sacred canopy,* which invests the meanings, faiths, and patterns of a culture with the authority of truth. See *Sacred Canopy: Elements of a Sociological Theory of Religion* (Garden City, N. Y.: Doubleday & Co., 1969).
12. Robert Bellah, "Epilogue: Religion and Progress in Modern Asia," *Religion and Progress in Modern Asia,* ed. Robert Bellah (New York: Free Press, 1965), p. 173.
13. For a discussion of religious diversity in the U.S. and responses to it, see E. Allen Richardson, *Strangers in This Land: Pluralism and the Response to Diversity in the United States* (New York: Pilgrim Press, 1988).
14. Albanese, *America Religions and Religion,* p. 7.
15. Berger, *Sacred Canopy,* pp. 94-101.
16. See Anthony F. C. Wallace, *Religion: An Anthropological View* (New York: Random House, 1966), pp. 30-51.
17. Latin American theologian Leonardo Boff calls the base-community movement the church's new reformation. See *Ecclesiogenesis: The Base Communities Reinvent the Church,* trans. Robert Barr (Maryknoll: Orbis Books, 1986).
18. See Andrew M. Greeley, *Religion: A Secular Theory* (New York: Free Press, 1982), pp. 49-51.
19. The image of night is significant. Anthropologists of religion call the ritual transitions when people are caught between meanings *liminal* moments. *Liminal* is a frightening, awesome, and vulnerable state, where old meanings are no longer adequate and new ones are not yet known. Metaphorically, liminal is the dark night of the soul. See Victor Turner, *The Ritual Process: Structure and Anti-structure,* Cornell Paperback Ed. (Ithaca: Cornell University Press, 1969), pp. 94-165; and Victor and Edith Turner, *Image and Pilgrimage in Christian Culture* (New York: Columbia University Press, 1978), pp. 1-39.
20. Clifford Geertz, *Interpretation of Cultures: Selected Essays* (New York: Basic Books, 1973), p. 90.

21. Paul Tillich, *Dynamics of Faith* (New York: Harper & Row Torchbook Ed., 1957), pp. 8-16. See also *What Is Religion?* trans. James Luther Adams (New York: Harper & Row, 1969).

22. Harold Kushner, *Who Needs God?* (New York: Pocket Books, 1989), p. 23.

23. Albanese, *American Religions and Religion,* pp. 8-9.

24. Theologian Avery Dulles calls these two functions the expository, communicating the contents of the faith as in a catechism; and the apologetic, presenting a faith to outsiders as "worthy of belief." See *The Communication of Faith and Its Content* (Washington, D.C.: The National Catholic Education Association, 1985), pp. 10-14. Peter L. Berger, *A Rumor of Angels: Modern Society and the Rediscovery of the Supernatural* (Garden City, N. Y.: Doubleday, Anchor Books, 1969); and David Tracy, *Blessed Rage for Order: The New Pluralism in Theology* (New York: Seabury Press, 1975) are examples of apologetic communication.

25. See Joseph V. Crockett, *Teaching Scripture from an African-American Perspective* (Nashville: Discipleship Resources, 1990). Two of the teaching strategies identified explicitly address these dimensions of religion. The Exile strategy is concerned with code; the sanctuary, with cultus.

26. Dulles, *Communication of Faith,* pp. 14-16. For a description of the role of community in Christian education, see Charles R. Foster, *Teaching in the Community of Faith* (Nashville: Abingdon Press, 1982).

27. For an explicit treatment of the educative dimensions of community, see Andrew M. Greeley and Mary Greeley Durkin, *How to Save the Roman Catholic Church* (New York: Viking Penguin, 1984).

28. Greeley, *Religious Imagination,* p. 17; see also pp. 10-20; and Greeley, *Religion,* pp. 161-63.

29. Many people understand religious education as referring only to the teaching of a particular religious content and the processes by which that content is "taught." This view is only one of several approaches to Christian education. For a description of five approaches see Jack Seymour and Donald Miller, eds., *Contemporary Approaches to Christian Education* (Nashville: Abingdon Press, 1982). The approach called "interpretation" is closest to the one we are developing in this book.

30. Greeley, *Religion,* p. 163; also see pp. 15-51.

Chapter 4: Living in the Intersections

1. Jack Mezirow, *Transformative Dimensions of Adult Learning* (San Francisco: Jossey-Bass, 1991), p. 35.

2. Ibid., p. 24.

3. James I. Loder, *The Transforming Moment: Understanding Convictional Experiences* (San Francisco: Harper & Row, 1981).

4. Richard A. Olson, "Toward 2001: Present Realities and Future Possibilities for Adult Education, Formation of Educators, and the Lay Ministry," *Religious Education* 84(Fall 1989):610.

5. Mary Elizabeth Moore, *Education for Continuity and Change: A New Model for Christian Religious Education* (Nashville: Abingdon Press, 1983), p. 111.

6. Cornel West, *Prophesy Deliverance!* (Philadelphia: Westminster Press, 1982), p. 17.

7. Henry James Young, *Hope in Process: A Theology of Social Pluralism* (Minneapolis: Fortress Press, 1990), p. 72.

8. Jurgen Moltmann, *The Passion for Life: A Messianic Lifestyle*, trans. and introduction, M. Douglas Meeks (Philadelphia: Fortress Press, 1978), p. 26.
9. For discussions of the personal being fulfilled only in community, see John Macmurray, *Persons in Relation* (New York: Harper & Brothers, 1961); and Frank Kirkpatrick, *Community: A Trinity of Models* (Washington, D.C.: Georgetown University Press, 1986).
10. Parker Palmer, *The Active Life: A Spirituality of Work, Creativity, and Caring* (San Francisco: Harper & Row, 1990), p. 17.
11. For a description of how education, as a method of critical reflection, affects both personal and social transformation, see Paulo Freire, *Pedagogy of the Oppressed*, trans. Myra Bergman Ramos (New York: Herder & Herder, 1972); and Ira Shor & Paulo Freire, *A Pedagogy for Liberation: Dialogues on Transforming Education* (South Hadley, Mass.: Bergin & Garvey, 1987).
12. Parker J. Palmer, *To Know As We Are Known: A Spirituality of Education* (San Francisco: Harper & Row, 1983), pp. 73-74.
13. Ibid., p. 74. For a further description of hospitality in religious education, see Linda Vogel, *Teaching and Learning in Communities of Faith: Empowering Adults Through Religious Education* (San Francisco: Jossey-Bass, 1991), pp. 93-110.
14. Henri Nouwen, *Reaching Out* (Garden City, N. Y.: Doubleday, 1975), p. 47. The relationship between hospitality and justice is explored in Anne Streaty Wimberly and Edward P. Wimberly, *Language of Hospitality: Intercultural Relations in the Household of God* (Nashville: Cokesbury, 1991).
15. See Yvonna S. Lincoln & Egon G. Guba, *Naturalistic Inquiry* (Beverly Hills: Sage Publications, 1985).
16. Brother Lawrence of the Resurrection, *The Practice of the Presence of God*, trans. and introduction, John J. Delaney (New York: Doubleday Image Book, 1977), p. 68.
17. Margaret A. Farley, *Personal Commitments: Beginning, Keeping, Changing* (San Francisco: Harper & Row, 1986), pp. 45-46, 55-66.
18. For a further description of practicing presence in religious education, see Charles R. Foster, *The Ministry of the Volunteer Teacher* (Nashville: Abingdon Press, 1986), pp. 52-58.
19. Palmer, *To Know As We Are Known*, p. 88.

Chapter 5: Havens of Hospitality

1. See Nathan Hare and Julia Hare, *Bringing the Black Boy to Manhood: The Passage* (San Francisco: The Black Think Tank, 1985); and Mary Lewis, *Herstory: Black Female Rites of Passage* (Chicago: African-American Images, 1988) which describe programs that link cultural criticism and personal growth.
2. Robert Bellah, Richard Madsen, William Sullivan, Ann Swidler, and Steven Tipton, *Habits of the Heart: Individualism and Commitment in American Life* (Berkeley: University of California Press, 1985), p. 62.
3. Eugene C. Roehlkepartain, *Exploring Educational Effectiveness. An Inventory for Congregational Leaders* (Minneapolis: Search Institute, 1990), p. 3. The full report is *Effective Christian Education: A National Study of Protestant Congregations—Project Summary* (Minneapolis: Search Institute, 1990).
4. Jean M. Haldane, *Religious Pilgrimage* (Washington, D.C.: Alban Institute, 1975).

5. Margaret Ann Durham [Crain], *An Ethnographic Study of Perspectives on Authority of Adult Sunday School Participants: Hearing the Voices* (Ed. D. dissertation, Vanderbilt University, 1991), p. 92. Our description of this class is drawn from this research.

6. Ibid., p. 102.

7. Ibid., p. 103.

8. Ibid., p. 105.

9. Ibid., p. 106.

10. Ibid., p. 107.

11. Ibid., p. 108.

12. Roehlkepartain, *Exploring Educational Effectiveness,* p. 25.

13. Stephen Schmidt, *Living with Chronic Illness: The Challenge of Adjustment* (Minneapolis: Augsburg, 1989), p. 73.

14. Ibid., p. 98.

15. Ibid.

16. Ibid., p. 96.

17. Ibid., pp. 98-99.

18. Malcolm L. Warford, *The Necessary Illusion: Church Culture and Educational Change* (Philadelphia: United Church Press, 1976), p. 11.

19. Craig Dykstra, "No Longer Strangers: The Church and Its Educational Ministry" 6(*Princeton Seminary Bulletin,* New Series, No. 3, 1985):189-99.

20. See James Gustafson, *Treasure in Earthen Vessels: The Church as a Human Community* (New York: Harper, 1961).

Chapter 6: Conversing at the Wall

1. For a description of the domestication of Christian religious education, see Jack L. Seymour, Robert T. O'Gorman, and Charles R. Foster, *The Church in the Education of the Public: Refocusing the Task of Religious Education* (Nashville: Abingdon Press, 1984).

2. Robert Bellah, Richard Madsen, William Sullivan, Ann Swindler, and Steven Tipton, *Habits of the Heart: Individualism and Commitment in American Life* (Berkeley: University of California Press, 1985), p. 277.

3. See Peter L. Berger and Richard John Neuhaus, *To Empower People: The Role of Mediating Structures in Public Policy* (Washington, D.C.: American Enterprise Institute for Public Policy Research, 1977).

4. Sidney E. Mead, *The Nation with a Soul of a Church* (New York: Harper & Row, 1975).

5. Bellah et al., *Habits of the Heart,* p. 221.

6. Surajit Sinha, "Religion in an Affluent Society," *Current Anthropology* 7(April 1966):190-93. See also Hervé Varenne, *Americans Together: Structured Diversity in a Midwestern Town* (New York: Teachers College Press, 1977), p. 55.

7. Bellah et al., *Habits of the Heart,* p. 224.

8. Lawrence A. Cremin, *Public Education* (New York: Basic Books, 1976), p. 50. See also Lawrence A. Cremin, *Popular Education and Its Discontents* (New York: Harper & Row, 1989).

9. See Edward T. Hall and Mildred Reed Hall, *Hidden Differences: Doing Business with the Japanese* (New York: Anchor Books, 1987).

10. Cremin, *Public Education,* p. 31.

11. John A. Hostetler and Gertrude Enders Huntington, *Children in Amish Society: Socialization and Community Education* (New York: Holt, Rinehart, & Winston, 1971).

12. See Robert T. O'Gorman, *The Church That Was a School: Catholic Identity and Catholic Education in the United States Since 1790* (Washington, D.C.: Catholic Education Futures Project, 1987), pp. 11-19; and Seymour, O'Gorman, and Foster, *Church in the Education of the Public,* pp. 67-89.

13. Maria Harris, *Fashion Me a People: Curriculum in the Church* (Louisville: Westminster/John Knox Press, 1989), pp. 68-70; and Elliott W. Eisner, *The Educational Act* (New York: Macmillan, 1979).

14. Cremin, *Public Education,* p. 96.

15. Ibid., p. 27.

16. Curriculum includes both the values a group seeks to influence and the processes it uses to teach.

17. Walter Brueggemann, *Interpretation and Obedience: From Faithful Reading to Faithful Living* (Minneapolis: Fortress Press, 1991), p. 43.

18. Ibid., p. 64.

19. Henry J. Young, *Hope in Process: A Theology of Social Pluralism* (Minneapolis: Fortress Press, 1990), p. 82.

20. "Doctrinal Standards and Our Theological Task," *The Book of Discipline of the United Methodist Church* (Nashville: The United Methodist Publishing House, 1988), pp. 77-86.

21. Andrew Greeley, *The Religious Imagination* (Los Angeles: Sadlier, 1981). See also Sallie McFague's discussion of metaphorical theology, *Models of God: Theology for an Ecological Nuclear Age* (Philadelphia: Fortress Press, 1987).

22. David Tracy and John B. Cobb, Jr., *Talking About God: Doing Theology in the Context of Modern Pluralism* (New York: Seabury Press, 1983), p. 2.

23. Parker Palmer, *The Active Life: A Spirituality of Work, Creativity, and Caring* (San Francisco: Harper & Row, 1990), p. 17.

24. Melanie Brubaker, "Carter Extolls Virtues of Volunteerism," *Columbia Daily Tribune* (October 1991), p. 1.

Chapter 7: Interpreting Among Interpreters

1. Mary Elizabeth Mullino Moore, *Teaching from the Heart: Theology and Educational Method* (Minneapolis: Fortress Press, 1991), p. 213.

2. Laurent Daloz, *Effective Teaching and Mentoring* (San Francisco: Jossey-Bass, 1987), p. 17.

3. For an analysis of this passage as transformatory learning, see James Loder, *The Transforming Moment: Understanding Convictional Experiences* (San Francisco: Harper & Row, 1981).

4. Moore, *Teaching from the Heart,* p. 200.

5. Rita Nakashima Brock, *Journeys by Heart: A Christology of Erotic Power* (New York: Crossroad, 1988), p. 22.

6. Parker J. Palmer, *To Know As We Are Known: A Spirituality of Education* (San Francisco: Harper & Row, 1983), p. 69.

7. Sallie McFague, "An Earthly Theological Agenda," *The Christian Century* 108(January 2-9, 1991):14.

8. Henry James Young, *Hope in Process: A Theology of Social Pluralism* (Minneapolis: Fortress Press, 1990), p. 78.

9. See Thomas Groome's focus on critical reflection, *Sharing Faith: A Comprehensive Approach to Religious Education and Pastoral Ministry. The Way of Shared Praxis* (San Francisco: HarperCollins, 1991); Charles Foster's attention to how ethnicity affects learning, *Ethnicity in the Education of the Church* (Nashville: Scarritt Press, 1987); and Mary Boys' attention to the ways the Bible has been used in teaching, *Biblical Interpretation in Religious Education* (Birmingham: Religious Education Press, 1980).

10. See Carol Gilligan, *In a Different Voice: Psychological Theology and Women's Development* (Cambridge: Harvard University Press, 1982); Carol Gilligan, Janie Victoria Ward, Jill McLean Taylor with Betty Bardige, eds., *Mapping the Moral Domain: A Contribution of Women's Thinking to Psychological Theory and Education* (Cambridge: Center for the Study of Gender, Education, and Human Development, Harvard University Graduate School of Education, 1988); Mary Belenky, Blythe M. Vicker Clinchy, Nancy Rule Goldberger, and Jill Mattuck Tarule, *Women's Ways of Knowing: The Development of Self, Voice, and Mind* (New York: Basic Books, 1986); Mary C. Lewis, *Herstory: Black Female Rites of Passage* (Chicago: African American Images, 1989); Nathan Hare and Julia Hare, *Bringing the Black Boy to Manhood: The Passage* (San Francisco: The Black Think Tank, 1985); and Foster, *Ethnicity in the Education of the Church.*

11. Discernment occurs in many ways. Jesus, for example, went to the wilderness, where through prayer and meditation he clarified his vocation. Theological reflection, prayer, meditation, and spiritual discernment are key means of discernment. In the Christian tradition, see Richard Foster, *Celebration of Discipline: The Path to Spiritual Growth* (New York: Harper & Row, 1978); Brian P. Hall, *Discerning* (Indianapolis: Center for the Exploration of Values and Meanings, 1977); and from another religious tradition, *The I Ching or Book of Changes*, 3rd ed., trans. Richard Wilhelm and Cary F. Baynes (Princeton: Princeton University Press, 1977).

12. The method of teaching described allows us to begin at any point in the threefold process. Teaching may move in any direction.

13. While the model assumes a community, an individual can use it in her or his own reflection and meditation.

14. Madeleine L'Engle, *A Circle of Quiet* (San Francisco: Harper & Row, 1972), pp. 120-21. The brackets indicate our interpretation of the quotation.

15. An image for teaching that begins with *discernment* is spiritual direction. See Barbara Troxell, "Soul Friends: The Role of Spiritual Directors," *The Christian Century* (March 4, 1992):245-47.

Chapter 8: Toward Wholeness with Justice

1. Jackson Carroll, Carl S. Dudley, and William McKinney, *Handbook for Congregational Studies* (Nashville: Abingdon Press, 1986), pp. 48-50.

2. Henry A. Giroux, *Teachers as Intellectuals: Toward a Critical Pedagogy of Learning* (Granby, Mass.: Bergin and Garvey, 1988), pp. 2-3.

3. John Macmurray, *Persons in Relation* (New York: Harper & Brothers, 1961), p. 17.

4. Frank Kirkpatrick, *Community: Trinity of Models* (Washington D.C.: Georgetown University Press, 1986), p. 169.

5. Dennis T. Jaffe, Cynthia D. Scott, and Ester M. Orioli, "Visionary Leadership: Moving a Company from Burnout to Inspired Performance,"

Transforming Leadership: From Vision to Results, ed. John D. Adams (Alexandria, Va.: Miles River Press, 1986), p. 97.

6. Robert J. Schreiter, *Constructing Local Theologies* (Maryknoll, N.Y.: Orbis Press, 1985), pp. 1-21. For a description of the role of vision in ministry, see Jackson W. Carroll, *Ministry as Reflective Practice: A New Look at the Professional Model* (Washington, D.C.: Alban Institute, 1986), pp. 8, 18, 25-29.

7. Jack Mezirow calls this response active reinterpretation: "We may either arrive at an interpretation that we are aware has gradually taken shape subconsciously, or we may be aware only that we are beginning to look at things differently"; see *Transformative Dimensions of Adult Learning* (San Francisco: Jossey-Bass, 1991), p. 104.

8. Giroux, *Teachers as Intellectuals,* pp. 2-10.

9. As with the teaching method, a leader can proceed with any of the three elements: exploring, considering, or discerning.

10. Donald Schoen, *The Reflective Practitioner: How Professionals Think in Action* (New York: Basic Books, 1988); Jackson Carroll, *Ministry as Reflective Practice*; and Robert T. O'Gorman, "The Search for a Usable Knowledge," *Religious Education* 83(Summer 1988):331-35.

11. Maria Harris, *Women and Teaching* (New York: Paulist Press, 1988).

12. Jack Seymour and Robert Moore, "Practical Hermeneutics and Religious Leadership: Implications for Theological Education," *Theological Field Education, Vol. IV, Practical Hermeneutics,* ed. Donald Beisswenger and Doran McCarty (San Francisco: Association for Theological Field Education, 1982), pp. 105-19.

13. Giroux, *Teachers as Intellectuals,* p. 125.

14. David Macmillan, *Sense of Community: An Attempt at Definition* (Nashville: Center for Community Studies, George Peabody College, 1976).

15. Edgar H. Schein, *Organizational Culture and Leadership* (San Francisco: Jossey-Bass, 1991), p. 96.

16. Schein describes four types of social space. *Intimate* distance refers to a proximity in which touching may occur. *Personal* distance refers to a space held between persons, as in a conversation. *Social* distance describes the space used to talk to several persons at once, as in speaking before a small group. *Public* distance pertains to persons more than twenty-five feet away and with less direct interaction. Ibid., pp. 96-98.

17. Stanley Aronowitz and Henry A. Giroux, *Postmodern Education: Politics, Culture, and Social Criticism* (Minneapolis: University of Minnesota Press, 1991), p. 115.

18. Craig Dykstra, "Reconceiving Practice," *Shifting Boundaries: Contextual Approaches to the Structure of Theological Education,* ed. Barbara G. Wheeler and Edward Farley (Louisville: Westminster/John Knox, 1991), p. 43. "Practice is participation in a cooperatively formed pattern of activity that emerges out of a complex tradition of interactions among many people sustained over a long period of time."

Postlude

1. John H. Vincent, "A Forward Look for the Sunday-School," *The Development of the Sunday-School, 1780–1905: The Official Report of the Eleventh*

International Convention (Boston: International Sunday-School Association, 1905), p. 166.

2. Paulo Freire, *Pedagogy of the Oppressed,* trans. Myra Bergman Ramos (New York: Continuum, 1985), p. 61.

3. Madeleine L'Engle, *The Glorious Impossible* (New York: Simon & Schuster, 1990), p. 1.

INDEX OF KEY CONCEPTS

Printed in the United States
27467LVS00006B/103